First World War
and Army of Occupation
War Diary
France, Belgium and Germany

38 DIVISION
115 Infantry Brigade
Royal Welsh Fusiliers
17th Battalion
4 December 1915 - 30 April 1919

WO95/2561/2

The Naval & Military Press Ltd
www.nmarchive.com
Published in association with The National Archives

Published by

The Naval & Military Press Ltd

Unit 10 Ridgewood Industrial Park,

Uckfield, East Sussex,

TN22 5QE England

Tel: +44 (0) 1825 749494

www.naval-military-press.com

www.nmarchive.com

This diary has been reprinted in facsimile from the original. Any imperfections are inevitably reproduced and the quality may fall short of modern type and cartographic standards.

© **Crown Copyright**
Images reproduced by permission of The National Archives, London, England, 2015.

Contents

Document type	Place/Title	Date From	Date To
Heading	WO95/2561/2 17 Battalion Royal Welsh Fusiliers.		
Heading	38th Division 115th Infy Bde. 17th Bn Roy Welch Fus Dec 1915-Apr 1919		
Heading	17th R. Welch Fus. Vol.2		
Heading	38th Div. 17th R.W. Fusiliers Vol. I. 121/7824 Dec 15 Apr.19		
War Diary	Winchester	04/12/1915	04/12/1915
War Diary	Havre.	05/12/1915	06/12/1915
War Diary	Aire.	07/12/1915	07/12/1915
War Diary	Blessy.	08/12/1915	20/12/1915
War Diary	Robecq.	21/12/1915	26/12/1915
War Diary	Laventie.	26/12/1915	31/12/1915
Miscellaneous	Strength on Landing at Havre.	05/12/1915	05/12/1915
Miscellaneous	Duty State for Week Ending.	11/12/1915	11/12/1915
Miscellaneous	Duty State for Week Ending.	18/12/1915	18/12/1915
Miscellaneous	Duty State for Week Ending.	25/12/1915	25/12/1915
War Diary	Laventie.	01/01/1916	02/01/1916
War Diary	Laventie and Hamet Billet.	03/01/1916	03/01/1916
War Diary	Hamet Billet.	04/01/1916	13/01/1916
War Diary	Reiz Bailleul & Trenches.	14/01/1916	14/01/1916
War Diary	Reiz Bailleul	14/01/1916	24/01/1916
War Diary	Vielle Chapelle	25/01/1916	31/01/1916
Miscellaneous	Duty State for Week Ending.	01/01/1916	01/01/1916
Miscellaneous	Duty State for Week Ending.	08/01/1916	08/01/1916
Miscellaneous	Duty State for Week Ending	15/01/1916	15/01/1916
Miscellaneous	Duty State for Week Ending	22/01/1916	22/01/1916
Miscellaneous	Duty State for Week Ending	29/01/1916	29/01/1916
Miscellaneous			
Heading	17th R.W. Fus. Vol. 3		
War Diary	Croix Barbee.	01/02/1916	17/02/1916
War Diary	Vielle Chapelle	18/02/1916	19/02/1916
War Diary	Festubert.	20/02/1916	27/02/1916
War Diary	Le Touret	28/02/1916	29/02/1916
Heading	17 R. Welsh Fus Vol. 4		
War Diary	Le Touret.	01/03/1916	06/03/1916
War Diary	Festubert.	07/03/1916	14/03/1916
War Diary	Le Touret	15/03/1916	15/03/1916
War Diary	Hingette	16/03/1916	27/03/1916
War Diary	Gorre	28/03/1916	06/04/1916
War Diary	Givenchy Village Line.	06/04/1916	08/04/1916
War Diary	Hingette.	09/04/1916	15/04/1916
War Diary	Fauqissart.	16/04/1916	18/04/1916
War Diary	Fauqissart & Laventie	19/04/1916	23/04/1916
War Diary	Fauqissart.	24/04/1916	26/04/1916
War Diary	Laventie	27/04/1916	30/04/1916
War Diary	Robermitz	01/05/1916	11/05/1916
War Diary	Trenches Moated Grange Sector.	12/04/1916	13/04/1916
War Diary	Riez Bailleul	14/05/1916	24/05/1916
War Diary	Robermetz	25/05/1916	04/06/1916
War Diary	Fauqissart.	05/06/1916	10/06/1916

Type	Location	Start	End
War Diary	Robermetz	11/06/1916	11/06/1916
War Diary	Robecq	12/06/1916	13/06/1916
War Diary	Auchel	14/06/1916	15/06/1916
War Diary	Chelers	16/06/1916	26/06/1916
War Diary	Neuvillette	26/06/1916	26/06/1916
War Diary	Longuevillette	27/06/1916	30/06/1916
Heading	115th Inf. Bde. 38th Div. War Diary 17th Battn. The Royal Welch Fusiliers. July 1916. Attached: Appendices.		
War Diary	Toutencourt	01/07/1916	01/07/1916
War Diary	Acheux	02/07/1916	03/07/1916
War Diary	Buire.	04/07/1916	05/07/1916
War Diary	Mametz	06/07/1916	13/07/1916
War Diary	Couin	14/07/1916	14/07/1916
War Diary	Coigneux.	15/07/1916	22/07/1916
War Diary	Courcelles.	23/07/1916	31/07/1916
Miscellaneous	Appendices.		
Miscellaneous	Special Order Of The Day By Major General Ivor Philipps, D.S.O. Commanding 38th (Welsh) Division.	05/07/1916	05/07/1916
Miscellaneous	Weekly Duty State For Week Ending July 2nd 1916	02/07/1916	02/07/1916
Miscellaneous	Weekly Duty State For Week Ending July 9th 1916	09/07/1916	09/07/1916
Miscellaneous	Weekly Duty State For Week Ending July 16th 1916	16/07/1916	16/07/1916
Miscellaneous	Weekly Duty State For Week Ending July 23rd 1916	23/07/1916	23/07/1916
Miscellaneous	Weekly Duty State For Week Ending 30th July 1916	30/07/1916	30/07/1916
War Diary	Watten Near St. Omer.	01/08/1916	02/08/1916
War Diary	Volkerinckhove	03/08/1916	10/08/1916
War Diary	Volkerinckhove Sheet 27 Belgium France G9 & 10	11/08/1916	16/08/1916
War Diary	Volkerinckhove	17/08/1916	19/08/1916
War Diary	Poperinghe.	19/08/1916	19/08/1916
War Diary	Ypres.	19/08/1916	29/11/1916
War Diary	Ypres Camp. G. Sheet 28 N.W. A.16.a.9.2	30/11/1916	04/12/1916
War Diary	G. Camp.	05/12/1916	08/12/1916
War Diary	Ypres	08/12/1916	31/12/1916
War Diary	Bollezeele	01/01/1917	14/01/1917
War Diary	Ypres (Popperinghe Camp G.).	15/01/1917	15/01/1917
War Diary	Ypres (Boesinghe L. Line).	16/01/1917	28/01/1917
War Diary	Boesinghe (Support Line)	29/01/1917	31/01/1917
War Diary	Ypres (Boesinghe Bleuet Farm. B.10.c.7.4).	01/02/1917	05/02/1917
War Diary	Boesinghe.	06/02/1917	12/02/1917
War Diary	Boesinghe (Bleuet FM.)	13/02/1917	17/02/1917
War Diary	Boesinghe.	17/02/1917	28/02/1917
War Diary	Ypres Boesinghe (Belgium 28 N.W. B.11b)	01/03/1917	02/03/1917
War Diary	X Camp (L.16.c.3.3)	03/03/1917	06/03/1917
War Diary	Bluet Farm B.10.C.3.3	06/03/1917	09/03/1917
War Diary	Boesinghe B.5.d.2.8	10/03/1917	13/03/1917
War Diary	X Camp A.16.c.3.3	14/03/1917	18/03/1917
War Diary	Elverdinghe (B.14 Control) to L.4 (H.12.a.4.5)	18/03/1917	20/03/1917
War Diary	Centre Section Canal Bank C.13.c.1.2	21/03/1917	31/03/1917
War Diary	Ypres VIII Corps. Left Div. Central Sect. (Zwaanhof).	01/04/1917	06/04/1917
War Diary	Centre Sect (Zwaanhof).	07/04/1917	09/04/1917
War Diary	'L' Line Elverdinghe (B.14 Central To H.12.a.4.5)	10/04/1917	10/04/1917
War Diary	L Line Elverdinghe B14 Central To L4 (H.12.a.45)	11/04/1917	19/04/1917
War Diary	Bleuet Farm B10.c.3.3	19/04/1917	26/04/1917
War Diary	Boesinghe B5.d.2.8	26/04/1917	30/04/1917
War Diary	Ypres VIII Corps. Left Div.	01/05/1917	01/05/1917
War Diary	Popperinghe Sheet 28 N.W.	02/05/1917	02/05/1917

Type	Location	From	To
War Diary	Millam F.28.a.7.6 (Sheet 27).	03/05/1917	15/05/1917
War Diary	Herzeele D. 10. b. 3.4	16/04/1917	17/04/1917
War Diary	Y Camp. Proven. F.7.b1.2	18/04/1917	18/04/1917
War Diary	Proven F.7.b.1.2	19/05/1917	23/05/1917
War Diary	Cardoen Fm (Sheet 28 N.W) A.18.a.8.7	24/05/1917	25/05/1917
War Diary	Cardoen Farm A.18.a.8.7	26/05/1917	12/06/1917
War Diary	Bleuet Fm. B.10.c.3.3	12/06/1917	14/06/1917
War Diary	X Line Extension	15/06/1917	27/06/1917
War Diary	Proven F.7.b.1.2	27/06/1917	27/06/1917
War Diary	Caestra P.3.6.b.	28/06/1917	28/06/1917
War Diary	Palfart	28/06/1917	30/06/1917
Operation(al) Order(s)	Operation Orders No. 29. By Lieut Col H.J. Taylor. Commanding 17th Battalion Royal Welsh Fusiliers.	11/06/1917	11/06/1917
Miscellaneous	Headquarters. 115 Inf. Bde.	01/08/1917	01/08/1917
War Diary	Palfart (Febin).	01/07/1917	15/07/1917
War Diary	Molinghem.	16/07/1917	16/07/1917
War Diary	Caestra	17/07/1917	17/07/1917
War Diary	Ecke	18/07/1917	18/07/1917
War Diary	Proven	19/07/1917	19/07/1917
War Diary	Seaton Camp (F.5.d.4.1).	20/07/1917	30/07/1917
War Diary	'H' Camp (A.9.C.8.7)	30/07/1917	31/07/1917
War Diary	Steenbeek.	01/08/1917	02/08/1917
War Diary	Canal Bank B.2.4.b.	02/08/1917	05/08/1917
War Diary	Elverdinghe.	05/08/1917	05/08/1917
War Diary	Seaton Camp (F.5.C.4.6).	06/08/1917	18/08/1917
War Diary	'H' Camp A.q.c.8.7	19/08/1917	28/08/1917
War Diary	'H' Camp.	28/08/1917	31/08/1917
War Diary	Malakoff Camp B.22.b.21 (St. Julien).	01/09/1917	04/09/1917
War Diary	Candle Cancer Trench (C.8.b.2.8).	04/09/1917	08/09/1917
War Diary	Candle Cancer Trench.	09/09/1917	09/09/1917
War Diary	Pala Camp.	09/09/1917	11/09/1917
War Diary	Eecke.	12/09/1917	12/09/1917
War Diary	Morbecque.	13/09/1917	13/09/1917
War Diary	Sailley Sur-La-Lys G22.b.2.8 Map 36	14/09/1917	14/09/1917
War Diary	Armentieres Sector.	15/09/1917	23/09/1917
War Diary	Houplines Sub-Sector.	23/09/1917	01/10/1917
War Diary	Armentieres Area.	02/10/1917	06/10/1917
War Diary	Houplines Sub-Sector.	07/10/1917	12/10/1917
War Diary	Armentieres Area.	13/10/1917	19/10/1917
War Diary	Houplines Sub-Sector.	19/10/1917	24/10/1917
War Diary	Armentieres Area. (in Reserve).	25/10/1917	30/10/1917
War Diary	Houplines Sub-Sector.	31/10/1917	06/11/1917
War Diary	Armentieres Area. (Reserve).	07/11/1917	07/11/1917
War Diary	Armentieres Area.	08/11/1917	09/11/1917
War Diary	Houplines Sub-Sector.	10/11/1917	16/11/1917
War Diary	Armentieres Area.	17/11/1917	22/11/1917
War Diary	Houplines Sub-Sector.	23/11/1917	30/11/1917
Miscellaneous	Headquarters 115 Inf. Bde.	01/01/1918	01/01/1918
War Diary	Houplines Sub-Sector.	01/12/1917	10/12/1917
War Diary	Laundries H.5.a.4.7	10/12/1917	14/12/1917
War Diary	Laundries.	14/12/1917	16/12/1917
War Diary	Houplines Sub-Sector.	17/12/1917	22/12/1917
War Diary	Estaires L.30.c.	23/12/1917	24/12/1917
War Diary	Estaires.	25/12/1917	31/12/1917
War Diary	Estaires L.30.o.c.	01/01/1918	06/01/1918
War Diary	Doulieu F.29.d.53.30	06/01/1918	13/01/1918

War Diary	Estaires L.30.c.	14/01/1918	13/02/1918
War Diary	Wez Macquart.	13/02/1918	31/03/1918
Heading	115th Inf. Bde. 38th Div. War Diary 17th Battn. The Royal Welch Fusiliers. April 1918		
War Diary		01/04/1918	01/04/1918
War Diary	Hedauville V.3.4.c.4.9	02/04/1918	13/04/1918
War Diary	Senlis V.16.b.8.8	14/04/1918	17/04/1918
War Diary	Bouzincourt W.13.a.9.9	18/04/1918	24/04/1918
War Diary	Bouzincourt W.13.a.9.9	25/04/1918	30/04/1918
War Diary	Bouzincourt.	01/05/1918	01/05/1918
War Diary	Senlis V.16.b.8.8	02/05/1918	08/05/1918
War Diary	Bouzincourt.	09/05/1918	22/05/1918
War Diary	Herrisart	23/05/1918	04/06/1918
War Diary	Divisional Reserve.	05/06/1918	06/06/1918
War Diary	Support Right Engle-Belmer.	07/06/1918	10/06/1918
War Diary	Front Line.	11/06/1918	12/06/1918
War Diary	Divisional Reserve Area Forceville.	13/06/1918	22/06/1918
War Diary	Mesnil Left Sector.	23/06/1918	28/06/1918
War Diary	Intermediary System Right.	29/06/1918	30/06/1918
Miscellaneous	HQ 115 Infy Bde.	02/08/1918	02/08/1918
War Diary	Intermediary System.	01/07/1918	08/07/1918
War Diary	Mesnil Left Sector.	09/07/1918	18/07/1918
War Diary	Herrisart.	19/07/1918	29/07/1918
War Diary	Acheux	30/07/1918	04/08/1918
War Diary	Bouzincourt.	05/08/1918	27/08/1918
War Diary	Feed.	29/08/1918	01/09/1918
War Diary	Morval.	01/09/1918	02/09/1918
War Diary	St. Martins Wood.	03/08/1918	05/08/1918
War Diary	Between Les Bouefs & Morval.	06/09/1918	09/09/1918
War Diary	Lechelle.	10/09/1918	16/09/1918
War Diary	Bde. Reserve.	17/09/1918	20/09/1918
War Diary	Le Transloy.	21/09/1918	28/09/1918
War Diary	Sorel Le Grande.	29/09/1918	03/10/1918
War Diary	Lemprie.	04/10/1918	04/10/1918
War Diary	Le Catalet	05/10/1918	05/10/1918
War Diary	Aubencheul Aux Bois.	06/10/1918	08/10/1918
War Diary	Villers Outreaux.	09/10/1918	10/10/1918
War Diary	Clary.	11/10/1918	12/10/1918
War Diary	Troisvillers.	13/10/1918	21/10/1918
War Diary	In The Line	22/10/1918	22/10/1918
War Diary	Troisvillers.	23/10/1918	23/10/1918
War Diary	Forest.	24/10/1918	26/10/1918
War Diary	Englefontaine	27/10/1918	29/10/1918
War Diary	Forest.	30/10/1918	02/11/1918
War Diary	Englefontaine.	03/11/1918	06/11/1918
War Diary	Aulnoye Station	07/11/1918	28/12/1918
War Diary	Engle Fontaine Inchy.	29/12/1918	31/12/1918
Miscellaneous	H Qrs 115 Inf Bde.	02/02/1919	02/02/1919
War Diary	Blangy Tronville.	01/01/1919	28/02/1919
Miscellaneous	To Hqrs 115 Inf. Bde.	31/03/1919	31/03/1919
War Diary	Blangy Tronville.	01/03/1919	30/04/1919

WO95/2561/2

17 Battalion Royal Welsh Fusiliers

38TH DIVISION
115TH INFY BDE

17TH BN ROY WELCH FUS
DEC 1915-APR 1919

17th R. Welch Thos.
Pt 2

2 £
13 sheet

35

115/38.

17th R.W. Franken
Vol: I

121/7824

38th K.w

Dec 15
Ap 16

I.P.
10 sheets

WAR DIARY
or
INTELLIGENCE SUMMARY

(Erase heading not required.)

Army Form C. 2118

Place	Date	Hour	Summary of Events and Information	Remarks and references to Appendices
Winchester	4.12.15		Paraded at 7.15 a.m. marched to SOUTHAMPTON. Entrained 13½ miles. Very wet. Arrived at Docks at 1 p.m. Battalion divided between 3 boats. Transport in one. 380 men under Captain C JONES in another. Skeard & nails and remainder in another. Sailed about 6 p.m. Very bad passage.	J.v.B
HAVRE	5"		Arrived at HAVRE and disembarked about 7 a.m. Stood near Transport park under Captain JONES did return. Marched to No 5 Rest Camp. Wet day.	J.v.B
"	6"		Park under Captain JONES arrived about 10 a.m. Battalion less 250 men paraded at 2 p.m. and entrained at HAVRE	J.v.B
AIRE	7"		Detrained at AIRE about 2.30 p.m. and marched to Billets in BLESSY and HAM. Distance about 3 miles. Very wet. We did not arrive till after dark.	J.v.B
BLESSY	8"		250 men of second party arrived about 1 a.m. Wet day. Spent day settling down.	J.v.B
"	9"		Wet day. Inspection and examining billets.	L.v.B
"	10"		Wet day. Scheme of training received from Brigade. Bombing musketry and Signalling instructors to be chosen at once	J.v.B

WAR DIARY
or
INTELLIGENCE SUMMARY

(Erase heading not required.)

Army Form C. 2118

Instructions regarding War Diaries and Intelligence Summaries are contained in F. S. Regs., Part II. and the Staff Manual respectively. Title Pages will be prepared in manuscript.

Place	Date	Hour	Summary of Events and Information	Remarks and references to Appendices
Blaringhem	20th	7.40am	The Batt. marched to new billets at ROBECQ, distance about 10 miles. Fine weather. Passed through the villages of 2nd Butt's who have been and seem the flagwaving of the war. Roads hard, condition of troops good.	Map Sheet 36 A.
ROBECQ	21st		Inspections, cleaning and repairing billets.	P.W. P.W.
"	22nd		Training under Coy arrangements. Bombing, rapid marching.	P.W.
"	23rd		Training under Coy arrangements, bombing classes, machine gun classes.	P.W.
"	24th		Inspections, route marching, instructional classes.	P.W.
"	25th		Xmas day – Church Parades – Welwrates provided. Received orders for move to trenches for instruction under 3rd Guards Brigade.	P.W.
"	26th	10am	Batt. moved by two and motor lorries to a point 1 mile from LAVENTIE and marched into LAVENTIE, then to be attached to 3rd Guards Brigade.	Map Sheet 36. P.W.

WAR DIARY or INTELLIGENCE SUMMARY

Army Form C. 2118

Place	Date	Hour	Summary of Events and Information	Remarks and references to Appendices
LAVENTIE	26th		Coys were allotted :— "A" Coy to 1st Grenadier Guards, "B" Coy to 4th Battn Grenadier Guards, "C" Coy to Gds Scots Guards, "D" Coy to 1st Battn Welsh Guards.	"A" Coy & "B" Coy PICANTIN "C" & D Coy FAUQISSART SHEET 36 1/40,000
— "—	27th		"A" & "D" Coys handed over trenches the same afternoon. "B" & "C" Coys remained in trenches. 1 killed in LAVENTIE.	P.W.
— "—	28th		A & D in trenches, B & C in killed.	(P.W.)
			1st Battn Grenadiers and 1st Welsh Guards relieved by 4th Grenadiers and Scots Guards respectively. A & D Coys to killed. B & C to trenches. Instruction in trenches very thorough. The standard of being with and observed though much appreciated by all ranks.	P.W.
— "—	29th		"B" & "C" Coys in trenches, "A" & "D" Coys in killed. Coys in killed.	P.W.
— "—	30th		"A" and "D" Coy to trenches. General clean up.	P.W.
— "—	31st		"A" and "D" Coy in trenches. B & C Coys in killed. Johnhund M.W.C	P.W.

Strength on landing at Havre

Battalion

29 Officers 6 W.Os. 4 Q.M.Sgts 40 Sgts
38 Cpls 39 Pd. Lance Corporals 18 L/Cpls
Lance Corporals 828 Men.

R.A.M.C.   1 Officer 1 Cpl. 4 Men
A.O.C.   1 Armr Sgt
A.S.C.   4 Drivers

17 Bn R.W.F.
5-12-15.

P. Welton Capt & Adjt
17/R. W. Fusiliers

Duty State for week ending 11th Decr. 1915.

Battn Strength:-

Officers	W.Os	CQMSgts	Sgts	Cpls	L/Cpls A.	L/Cpls U/p	Men
29	5	4	40	38	39	19	828

Attached

RAMC

| 1 | - | - | - | 1 | - | - | 4 |

AOC

| - | - | - | 1 | - | - | - | - |

ASC

| - | - | - | - | - | - | - | 4 |

Interpreter

| - | - | - | - | - | - | - | 1 |

Hospital
Entered during week   7 men
Discharged   "   1 "
Left in Hospl. Dec 11th   6 "

P. Welton Capt & Adjt
7/R. W. F.

Duty State for week ending 18th Decr 1915.

Battalion

	Officers	WOs	2MS&b	Sgts	L/Sgts	Cpls	L/Cpls	W/pte/gl	Men
	29	6	4	40	-	38	39	18	828

Attached.

RAMC	1	-	-	-	-	1	-	-	4
AOC	-	-	-	1	-	-	-	-	-
Interpreter	-	-	-	-	-	-	-	-	1
ASC	-	-	-	-	-	-	-	-	4

Hospital

Entered during week   10 men
Discharged   "   "   - "
Left in Hospital on Dec 18th   16 "

P. Welton Capt & Adjt
17/R.W.F.

Duty State for week ending 25th Decr 1915.

Battalion

Officers	WOs	2nd Sgts	Sgts	A/Sgts	Corpls	A/Corpls	L/Cpls	Men
29	6	4	41	8	34	51	32	799

(Note:- One A/L/Cpl was reduced Dec 22nd. Establishment completed to date 4-12-15.)

Attached

RAMC	1	-	-	-	-	-	-	-	4
AOC	-	-	-	1	-	-	-	-	-
Interpreter	-	-	-	-	-	-	-	-	1
ASC	-	-	-	-	-	-	-	-	4

(Note:- RAMC Corpl reduced to ranks by F.G.C.M and returned to 129th Field Ambulance.)

Hospital.

Entered during week   1 officer   11 men.
Discharged   -   -   6 men
Left in Hospital 25th Dec   1 officer   21 men.

P. Welson Capt & Adjt
17/R.W.F.

WAR DIARY
or
INTELLIGENCE SUMMARY
(Erase heading not required.)

Army Form C. 2118

Instructions regarding War Diaries and Intelligence Summaries are contained in F. S. Regs., Part II. and the Staff Manual respectively. Title Pages will be prepared in manuscript.

Place	Date	Hour	Summary of Events and Information	Remarks and references to Appendices
LAVENTIE	1916 1st Jan		"B" and "C" Coys to trenches with orders to relieve "A" & "D" Coys to billets.	
		11.30am	Enemy shelled Battalion Hd Qtrs but beyond knocking a few tiles off no damage was done. Orders for defences of trenches received.	P.W.
	2nd Jan		"A" & "D" Coys in billets. "B" & "C" Coys relieved from trenches in the evening ready for defences next day.	P.W.
LAVENTIE AND HAMET BILLET	3rd Jan	12.30pm	Battalion marched out of LAVENTIE to a point one mile away, and proceeded by two and three lorries to billets at HAMET BILLET about 2 miles from Battalion arrived there about 4.30 pm. Billets had already been allotted and the Battalion was settled down by 4.30 pm.	SHEET 36A
			The period in the front line covered 8 days during which time the trenches of "C" and "D", to which the regiment was attached, did all in their power to keep in the construction of all ranks, and the good feeling and camaraderie was most marked.	P.W.
HAMET BILLET	4th Jan		The Medical Officer of the battalion held an inspection, no cases of frostbite or chilled feet were discovered. Inspection of kit, equipment and clothing by O.C. Coys.	P.W.

1875 Wt. W593/826 1,000,000 4/15 J.B.C. & A. A.D.S.S./Forms/C. 2118.

Army Form C. 2118

WAR DIARY
or
INTELLIGENCE SUMMARY
(Erase heading not required.)

Place	Date	Hour	Summary of Events and Information	Remarks and references to Appendices
HAMLET BILLET	5/7/		Battalion in training. General march out and allotment for drill, bomb throwing etc.	P.W.
	6/7/		Brigadier General Evans inspected the Battalion on parade at ROBECQ. After inspection of the battalion in mass, Coys were inspected at drill, bayonet fighting etc. The Battalion took movers made an attack on enemy trenches and have bombs, and a party would investigate in my A? patrol work carried out a successful scheme in the evening.	P.W.
	7/7/		Battalion in training.	P.W.
	8/7/		Route march with the object of informing minor tactics and to increase powers of endurance of the men.	P.W.
	9/7/		Battalion allotted baths in the brewery at ROBECQ to the great satisfaction of the men. Church Parade — voluntary for the wood part on account of men being at baths.	P.W.
	10/7/ 11/7/		Battalion in training. The 11th Corps Army Corps Cmdr (General Haking) held a conference at ROBECQ, & spoke to a proportion of officers from each unit in the 38th Div. All of which were much appreciated. Battalion in training. regained in the 38th Div: — motivation & much appreciated.	P.W.

WAR DIARY or INTELLIGENCE SUMMARY

Army Form C. 2118

Place	Date	Hour	Summary of Events and Information	Remarks and references to Appendices
HAMET-BILLET.	11th		Battalion in training; practise with gas helmets carried out.	P.W.
	12th		Battalion in training. C.O., O.C. Coys and Coy Sgt Majors proceeded to the trenches to reconnoitre position and to inspect forward billeting area at REIZ BAILLEUL, a small village near LAVENTIE SHEET 36.	P.W. P.N.
	13th	10am	Battalion marched to REIZ BAILLEUL via ROBECQ, CALONNE, LA BASSEE CANAL, FOSSE, and BOUT DEVILLE (Sheet 36A). Settled in new billets by 11.30 am. Relieved 10th Battn Welch Regt in billets.	P.N.
REIZ BAILLEUL & TRENCHES	14th		Battalion relieved 13th Welch Regt in trenches, the night resting on a front about 1 mile N.of Neuve Chapelle, the scene of a big action in the early spring of 1915. The line included the notorious "Duck's Bill" - a maze of trenches jutting out from the main line and formerly a system of Germann communication trenches. "C" Coy occupied this part of the line i.e. the RIGHT, "D" Coy the Centre, and "A" Coy the LEFT. "B" Coy was in supporting points behind the front line. System of relief, 48 hours in front line, 48 hours	P.W.

WAR DIARY
or
INTELLIGENCE SUMMARY
(Erase heading not required.)

Army Form C. 2118

Place	Date	Hour	Summary of Events and Information	Remarks and references to Appendices
REIZ BAILLEUL	14/5		in Reserve billet at REIZ BAILLEUL.	P.W.
	15/5		Battalion in trenches.	P.W.
	16/5		Relieved from trenches in evening by 16th Welsh Regt, casualties during 48 hours, 1 killed, 2 wounded. This was the Battalion's first experience of holding the line, the reliefs were well carried out, and confidence in itself is increased to a great extent in the Battalion.	
	17/5		In billets. Inspections of Arms, ammunition & equipment, clothing etc.	P.W.
	18/5		Chaplain attached to the Brigade held voluntary church service. Battalion prepared for trenches in the evening. Relieved 16th Welsh Regt in trenches.	P.W.
	19/5		In trenches. Demonstration against enemy front line by continued artillery & infantry fire. Enemy retaliated in "Duck's bill" causing casualties. 1 Officer wounded, 3 other ranks killed and nine wounded.	P.W. Wounded Lieut F.L.? [illegible]
	20/5		In trenches, relieved in the evening by 16th Welsh regt	P.W.

Army Form C. 2118			
WAR DIARY **INTELLIGENCE SUMMARY** *(Erase heading not required.)*			
Place	Date	Hour	Summary of Events and Information	Remarks and references to Appendices

Place	Date	Hour	Summary of Events and Information	Remarks and references to Appendices
REIZ BAILLEUL	21st		Battalion in billets. One Company allotted baths at Pont du Hem.	Sheet 36. P.W.
	22nd		Battalion in billets, inspection in morning, moved to trenches in evening to relieve 16th Welch regt. 3 Coys allotted baths in morning, much appreciated by the men. Baths very well run & organized, clean clothing served out to men after bathing etc.	P.W.
	23rd		In the trenches. Captain Bleddyn Williams 2nd in command of "B" Coy went out with a patrol of 1 Sgt & 1 Pte during the night. The last touch with this patrol and did not return. Search was made by patrols throughout the night but nothing more discovered of the missing officer. Casualties. One Sergeant killed, 1 man wounded.	P.W. P.W.
	24th		In the trenches. Casualties 3 men wounded.	P.W.
VIELLE CHAPELLE	25th	11 am	In the trenches, relieved in the evening by the 1st Battn Irish Guards, and returned to REIZ BAILLEUL. Battn relieved from Brigade reserve by 2nd Battn Grenadier guards and marched to VIELLE CHAPELLE where they went into Divisional Reserve.	Sheet 36A R 34.a. P.W.

WAR DIARY or INTELLIGENCE SUMMARY

Army Form C. 2118

(Erase heading not required.)

Place	Date	Hour	Summary of Events and Information	Remarks and references to Appendices
VIEILLE CHAPELLE	Jan. 26th		Battalion in training. Bombing range erected, billets improved. Inspection of equipment, clothing etc. reefitting. Baths for N.C.O's & men. Talk was posted on phosphorus behind firing line. These posts are in the nature of "keeps", the idea of establishing them is to deny a surprise on the enemy should he succeed in breaking the 1st line of trenches. Each post is self supporting and a permanent garrison which is increased by reserves detachments in the event of attack, and has its own supply of ammunition, rations, materiel for repairs etc.	
	27th		Battalion in training. Baths for N.C.O's & men. Practice with gas helmets. Working parties formed for improving communication trenches at rear of the lines. 1 Officer wounded whilst in charge of one of these parties.	P.W.
	28th		Battalion in training.	P.W. ⚔ Lieut Morgan Wilbeam
	29th		Battalion in training.	
	30th		Church Parade in am and Colonel VIEILLE CHAPELLE. Saw Minister of Munitions in the afternoon.	P.W. P.W.

WAR DIARY
or
INTELLIGENCE SUMMARY

Army Form C. 2118

Place	Date	Hour	Summary of Events and Information	Remarks and references to Appendices
NEELLE CHAPELLE	Jan 31st	5 pm	Battalion moved into billets in Brigade reserve at CROIX BARBEE.	Sheet 36. P.W.
CROIX BARBEE	Feb 1st			

J. A. Bethune W. W.

Duty State for week ending 1st Jan 1916

Battalion Strength

	Officers	WOs	NCOs	Men	Total
A Coy	6	3	21	221	251
B Coy	6	1	21	216	244
C Coy	6	1	22	229	258
D Coy	6	1	21	216	244
Hdqrs Officers	5	-	-	-	5
	29	6	85	877	997
Attached RAMC	1	-	1	4	6
A.O.C.	-	-	1	-	1
A.S.C.	-	-	-	4	4

Strength of Battalion at Laventie

	Officers	WOs	NCOs	Men	Total
Hdqrs. Officers	5	-	-	-	5
A Coy	5	2	17	176	200
B Coy	4	1	15	176	196
C Coy	5	1	20	193	219
D Coy	5	1	20	192	218
Total	24	5	72	737	838

Sick in Hospital

	1	-	1	40	42

Wounded in Hospital

	-	-	-	1	1

Duty State for week ending 8th Jan 1916

Battalion Strength

	Officers	WOs	NCOs	Men	Total
A Coy	6	3	21	219	249
B Coy	6	1	21	214	242
C Coy	6	1	22	229	258
D Coy	6	1	21	215	243
Hdqrs Officers	5				5
	29	6	85	877	997
Attached R.A.M.C.	1	-	1	4	6
AOC	-	-	1	-	1
ASC	-	-	-	4	4

Sick
Entered Hospital during week — 40 OR.
Discharged from Hospital during week — 11 OR.
Left in Hospital on Jan 8th — 1 Officer 60 OR.

Wounded
In Hospital — 1

Duty State for week ending 15th January 1916

	Officers	WOs	NCOs	Men	Total
Battalion Strength	5				5
A Coy.	6	3	21	219	249
B Coy	6	1	21	214	242
C Coy.	6	1	22	229	258
D Coy	6	1	21	214	242
Total	29	6	85	876	996
Attached					
R.A.M.C.	1	-	1	4	6
A.V.C.			1	-	1
A.S.C.				4	4
In Hospital					
A Coy				13	13
B Coy			2	10	12
C Coy	1		2	23	26
D Coy			1	15	16
Total	1	-	5	61	67

Duty State for week ending 22nd January 1916.

Battalion Strength	Officers	W.Os	N.C.Os	Men	Total
Headquarters Officers	5				5
A Coy	6	3	22	218	249
B Coy	6	1	21	214	242
C Coy	6	1	22	226	255
D Coy	6	1	21	214	242
Total	29	6	86	872	993
Attached					
R.A.M.C.	1		1	4	6
A.O.C.			1		1
A.S.C.				4	4

In Hospital					
A Coy.				15	15
B Coy.			1	9	10
C Coy.	2		3	26	31
D Coy.			2	14	16
Total	2	-	6	64	72

Duty State for Week ending 29th January 1916.

	Officers	WOs.	NCOs.	Men	Total
Battalion Strength.					
Headquarter Officers	5	-	-	-	5
A Coy	5	3	21	217	241
B Coy	5	1	21	214	236
C Coy	6	1	21	226	248
D Coy	6	1	22	218	241
Total.	27	6	85	875	971
Attached					
R.A.M.C	1	-	1	4	5
A.O.C	-	-	1	-	1
A.S.C.	-	-	-	4	4
In Hospital.					
A Coy	-	-	-	16	16
B Coy	-	-	2	10	12
C Coy	2	-	4	27	33
D Coy	1	-	-	15	16
Total.	3	-	6	68	77

115

17th R.W. Fus:
vol: 3

WAR DIARY or INTELLIGENCE SUMMARY

Army Form C. 2118

Place	Date	Hour	Summary of Events and Information	Remarks and references to Appendices
CROIX BARBEE	1916 Feb 1st		Battalion in Brigade reserve billets in forward areas.	Sheet 36 P.W.
	2nd		Battalion in billets. Training, Machine gun class, bombing etc. Baths arranged for N.C.O's and men.	P.W.
	3rd		Batt'n in billets. Training carried out. Orders received for move to trenches on 4th inst.	P.W.
	4th		Battalion relieved 16th Welsh Regt in trenches about NEUVE CHAPPELLE in the evening. Relief well carried out. Trenches in a much better condition than had been expected, but considerable room for improvement. G.O.C. decided to alter the 48 hour relief into relief of 4 days. Three Coys in front line & 1 Coy in support. Casualties for first 24 hours, 1 man wounded.	
	5th		Battalion in trenches. Casualties 2 men wounded.	P.W.
	6th		Battalion in trenches. Casualties 2 men wounded.	P.W.
	7th		Battalion in trenches.	P.W.

WAR DIARY
or
INTELLIGENCE SUMMARY

(Erase heading not required.)

Army Form C. 2118

Place	Date	Hour	Summary of Events and Information	Remarks and references to Appendices
CROIX BARBEE	8th		Battalion in trenches. Relieved in the evening by 16th Welsh Regt. A most satisfactory relief, all ranks showing steady and marked improvement. A large amount of good work done in the trenches, and owing to the longer time spent there all ranks were able to and appreciate their work, more so then when doing 48 hour reliefs. Hot tea served out to the men on return to trenches.	P.W.
	9th		Batt. in Brigade reserve billets. Day spent in cleaning up, arms ammunition, equipment & clothing inspected and overhauled.	P.W.
	10th		Batt. in billets. Refitting etc. Arrested 16th Welsh Regt in getting trench material up to trenches. Major Walker Batt. in billets, working parties drawing	P.W. Colonel Ballard proceeded on leave. P.W.
	11th			P.W.

WAR DIARY
or
INTELLIGENCE SUMMARY
(Erase heading not required.)

Army Form C. 2118

Place	Date	Hour	Summary of Events and Information	Remarks and references to Appendices
CROIX BARBEE	Feb 12th		Battalion in billets, relieved 16th Bn Welsh Regt in the evening. Relief well carried out. Lieut D.O. Evans was killed behind the line by a stray bullet. He was buried next day at St VAAST.	✱ BETHUNE (continued) M32, C.9-8. P.W.
	13th		Battalion in trenches, casualties 4 N.C.O's men wounded.	P.W.
	14th		Battalion in trenches, three young officers reported their arrival and were posted to Coys, "A" Coy taking two and "C" Coy, one. Casualties nil.	P.W.
	15th		Batt in trenches. Orders for relief on 16th received. Casualties 2 O. ranks killed, 3 O. ranks wounded.	P.W.
	16th		Batt relieved in trenches by 7th Batt E. Lancashire Regt. Relief smartly carried out. Officers & men show improvement with each tour in the trenches. Batt marched to billets in CROIX BARBEE then to farm in the night.	P.W.
	17th		Batt relieved in Brigade Reserve at 11am by 7th / 13th Kings Own Lancaster Regt, and marched to billets at VIELLE CHAPELLE	P.W.

WAR DIARY or INTELLIGENCE SUMMARY

Army Form C. 2118

Place	Date	Hour	Summary of Events and Information	Remarks and references to Appendices
VIEILLE CHAPELLE	Feb: 18th		Orders for move to new area cancelled for this day. Spent the day in inspection, clothing and refitting, cleaning up of men and billets. 2/Lieut Kumblu reported his arrival from 19th Hussars.	P.W. BETHUNE Combined Sheet R.34.a.
	19th		A billeting party left at 9am to take over new billets near FESTUBERT, the scene of an offensive action by the British troops in May 1915. Battalion marched to new billets at 4 pm. Distance about 4 miles, and was settled down by 6 pm. Relieved the 17½ Batt? Middlesex reg?.	P.W.
FESTUBERT	20th		In billets. Fatigues carried out to assist in the improving of the line generally. A gas alarm came from the Brigade on the RIGHT (113th B.de) which eventually proved to be false. The Batt? stood to arms with gas helmets ready. "Stand down" was ordered by the Brigade at 8.40 pm. Although the alarm was false, it proved excellent practice for all ranks. The turn out was correct and along. A Coy of 18th Lancs Fusiliers (Bantams) arrived for instruction (Capt Wilkinson in command)	MAP reference BETHUNE (Trench Sheet) Edition 6. S 19 to 25. P.W.
	21st		Batt? in billets, fatigues, inspection and cleaning up.	P.W.

WAR DIARY or INTELLIGENCE SUMMARY

Army Form C. 2118

Place	Date	Hour	Summary of Events and Information	Remarks and references to Appendices
FESTUBERT	22nd		Battalion in billets. Colonel Ballard returned from leave. O.C. Coys & a proportion of Officers & N.C.O's proceeded to the trenches to reconnoitre the positions to be held by them and the best way of reaching same.	P.W.
	23rd		Batt'n in billets. relieved 16th Batt'n Welch regt in trenches. Disposition:- 2 Platoons of "A" Coy, 2 Platoons of "B" Coy in front line. $ "10" Platoon of A, B, C + D Coys in OLD BRITISH LINE. 2 Platoons of "D" Coy in reserve in FESTUBERT village. The front line at the present time consists merely of redoubts, communications with which can only be got at night time. The ground is in a bad state and any attempt to dig or build is promptly stopped by the enemy who is apt to be rather too attentive at this place. Heavy falls of snow followed by sharp frost have been the outstanding feature of the weather the last few days. Received 9 cadets for instruction. Casualties for 24 hours - nil -	P.W.

WAR DIARY or INTELLIGENCE SUMMARY

Army Form C. 2118

Place	Date	Hour	Summary of Events and Information	Remarks and references to Appendices
FESTUBERT	24th		Battalion in the trenches. The men of the 18th Lancashire Fusiliers accompanied the Battn. and a proportion each night were put into the dugouts for instruction.	P.W.
	25th		Battn. in the trenches. 2/Lieut Lance from the 12th Reserve Battn. reported for duty.	P.W.
	26th		Battn. in the trenches. System of providing hot soup for the men experimented on & found satisfactory.	P.W.
	27th		Battn. in the trenches. The Medical Officer (Lieut Thomas) having completed his one years engagement, left the Battn. & was succeeded by Capt Walsh R.A.M.C. Relieved in the evening by the 16th Welsh Regt. Reinforcements from England continued — 40 men. Battn. marched to billets at LE TOURET.	P.W. BETHUNE continued Sheet X 16 B + D.
LE TOURET	28th		Battn. in billets. Inspection of Arms, clothing & accoutrements. No cases of frostbite or "trench feet" occurred during tour in the trenches, despite the frosty weather, which the Battn's arrangements for billets, hot baths for the Battn's mind appreciated.	P.W.
	29th			P.W.

[signature]

38

17 R Welsh
Fus
Vol 4

H.P.
10 chuds

WAR DIARY or INTELLIGENCE SUMMARY

Army Form C. 2118

17 R.W.F.

Place	Date	Hour	Summary of Events and Information	Remarks and references to Appendices
LE TOURET.	MARCH 1st		Battalion in billets. A concert was held in the evening to celebrate St. David's day. The Commg Officer afterwards addressed the men, thanking them for their conduct at Ypres & Cuinchy. He quoted a Telegram with piece of work performed by the 2nd Battn of the Regiment on 5th Feb in which resulted in the capture and consolidation of a German position. The officers of the Battn. dined together in the evening.	
	2nd		Baths were allotted to a portion of the Battn. in the morning. Relieved 16th Welsh Regt in the trenches in the evening.	
	3rd		In the trenches. 2nd Lieut Allen was killed by a sniper whilst examining the enemy position over the top of the parapet. Other casualties 11 men killed and two wounded.	
	4th		Battn in trenches. Casualties 1 killed, 1 wounded.	
	5th		Battn in trenches.	
	6th		Battn. in trenches. Casualties 1 killed (1)/R.W.F.) 1 killed 14th Gloster Regt attached for instruction. Relieved in the evening by 16th Welsh Regt. Returned to billets in FESTUBERT.	

Army Form C. 2118.

WAR DIARY
or
INTELLIGENCE SUMMARY
(Erase heading not required.)

Place	Date	Hour	Summary of Events and Information	Remarks and references to Appendices
FESTUBERT	March 7th		Battn in billets. During the period 27th Feb to 7th March the 14th Battn Gloucester Regt were attached for instruction. They left on this date having completed their instruction.	
	8th		Battn in billets. Baths supplied to Battn, a thing always much appreciated by the men.	
	9th		A "Flammenwerfer" demonstration was given at Divl H.Q. with captured German apparatus. Several officers attended and were much interested.	
	10th		Relieved the 16th Welch Regt in trenches. Weather conditions much improved and a decided fall of water noticed from our previous turn in trenches. Fair weather prevailed. Casualties 1 wounded.	
	11th		Battn in trenches.	
	12th		Battn in trenches.	
	13th		Battn in trenches.	
	14th		Battn in trenches. Casualties 1 killed, 3 wounded. The 15th Stafford Fusiliers who had been attached for instruction were 7th and left the Battn on completion of training. Relieved in the evening by 16th Welch Regt and proceeded to Billets at LE TOURET.	

WAR DIARY or INTELLIGENCE SUMMARY

Army Form C. 2118.

Place	Date	Hour	Summary of Events and Information	Remarks and references to Appendices
LE TOURET	15th		Batt^n marched to HINGETTE to Divisional Reserve. Distance about 5 miles. All arrived in new billets by 12.30 p.m. During the night (14-15th), one man died in billets.	X Bethune Contoured Sheet W. 16 c.
HINGETTE	16th		Batt^n in billets. Inspection, refitting, arms and accoutrements checked. Thorough cleaning up & getting rid of accumulated dirt from trench life.	
	17th		Batt^n in billets. A draft of 2 officers and 55 O. Ranks arrived from England. Strong working parties found for strengthening defences of rear line.	
	18th		Batt^n in billets. The R.B. football team played a match with the 10th S.W.B. Cooking classes formed.	
	19th		Bombing classes, outing t. M. Gunners training. Church Parades in fields by-joining billets.	
	20th		Batt^n in billets. batho arranged for whole battalion.	
	21st		C.O. inspected Coys in billets.	
	22nd		Batt^n in billets. Inspection of trench warfare. Parties in billets. Inspection of Battalion by Brig. General Evans. O.C. Coys inspected the new line of trenches at GIVENCHY.	

WAR DIARY or INTELLIGENCE SUMMARY

Army Form C. 2118.

Place	Date	Hour	Summary of Events and Information	Remarks and references to Appendices
HINGETTE	23rd March		Battn left billets, after a very pleasant & welcome rest, at 11 a.m. and marched into the forward area at GIVENCHY village. Billeted the night in the ruins of GIVENCHY village.	BETHUNE Contoured Sheet, Square A9
	24th		Relieved the 9th Battn Welch Regt in the trenches, disposing 3 Coys in line, 1 Coy in Support in the village near PONT FIXE. Right of Battn rested on LA BASSEE Canal. 33rd Division on trenches on our RIGHT, 10th S.W.B. on our LEFT. Relief worked well & no casualties during the operation.	
	25th		In the trenches. Enemy sprang a mine in front of our LEFT Coy causing 13 casualties, one of whom died. Total Casualties for 24 hours, 1 died of wounds 8. O.ranks wounded. Owing to a slight error in the report on mine crater, the Division issued attached instructions.	Appendix I.
	26th		Battn in trenches. Casualties 10. ranks wounded. All ranks in front line shew a decided keenness in anything. Reserves in the use of Rifle grenades.	
	27th		Hostile artillery much more active, shelling our front line & communicating trenches heavily. Considerable from trenches fair — much need.	

WAR DIARY
INTELLIGENCE SUMMARY

Army Form C. 2118.

Place	Date 1916	Hour	Summary of Events and Information	Remarks and references to Appendices
GORRE.	Mar 28		Battalion in the trenches. Casualties. Nil. Relieved by 16th Batt. Welsh Regt. Relief commenced 1 p.m. Batt. marched by Platoons to Reserve Billets at GORRE CHATEAU. Batt. in Billets 6 p.m.	BETHUNE. Contoured Sheet F 3 b
	" 29		Battalion in Billets. Bath allotted Batt. Inspection by Medical Officer. Capt Welton (Adjutant) and Lieut A. Jones proceeded on leave. by v. 19 a.m. train from Bethune.	
	" 30		Battalion in Billets. Armourer Sgt inspects arms at Coy. Inspection of Gasshelmets, Rifles & Ammunition. Batt. employed on fatigue work. — making Sandbagging during evening for Engineers.	
	" 31		Battalion in Billets. Practice in dummy and live bomb throwing, gasshelmet practice. and more fatigue parties found.	

La Bethune Rels.

WAR DIARY or INTELLIGENCE SUMMARY

17. R. Welsh Fus
Army Form C. 2118
Vol 5

Place	Date	Hour	Summary of Events and Information	Remarks and references to Appendices
GORRE	1916 April 1		Battalion leaves Billets for the trenches - Right subsector, Givenchy line. Relief commencing at 1.30 p.m. Complete 5 p.m. Casualties Nil	Bethune Combined Sheet A.9 +15
	2		Battalion in the trenches. Casualties Nil	
	3		Ditto	
			Mine sprung by enemy on the left of our sector, causing some damage. No right of 11th S.W.B. line. Casualties Killed 1. O.R. Wounded 5. Enemy taking the W with Cottonwood gas attack anticipated, but did not ensue. Both in the trenches. Casualties Nil	
			Both relieved by 16th Welsh Regt. Relief commenced at 1 p.m. completed at 3 p.m. Batt. occupied support trench in the VILLAGE LINE. R.S.M. Albert. Casualties 2 O.R. wounded.	6 M
		4.50		
	6		Capt Loft Jones went on leave.	5 P 9 white

WAR DIARY
or
INTELLIGENCE SUMMARY
(Erase heading not required.)

Army Form C. 2118

Place	Date 1916	Hour	Summary of Events and Information	Remarks and references to Appendices
GIVENCHY VILLAGE LINE.	April 6		Battalion in support Billets. Engaged on R.E. fatigue work. Battalion in Support Billets. Relief when received.	BETHUNE enlarged sheet. SA 9.
	7			
	8		Battalion relieved in VILLAGE LINE by 15th Battn A.I.F. Relief commenced at 10.30 am, but delayed owing to the enemy shelling ESTAMINET CORNER. Brigadier Genl inspected the billets about noon. Relief recommenced about 1.30 pm, and was completed at 4 pm. Battn marched off by Coys to NINGETTE and was in billets by about 9 pm. Aeroplane telegram from R.F. Corps received from Division reports that information received of BOIS DE BIEZ from M30A to S16A is covered by what looks like single broad planks about every 6 feet.	
NINGETTE	9		Battn in Billets. Sunday Church of England service 11.30 am. New Com 11am. Sq W16. Battn allotted Baths at ESSARS.	

WAR DIARY
or
INTELLIGENCE SUMMARY

(Erase heading not required.)

Army Form C. 2118

Place	Date	Hour	Summary of Events and Information	Remarks and references to Appendices
HINGETTE	1916 Ap 10		Batt. in billets. Cleaning up. Inspection of A & B Coys by C.O. Warning of enemy activity infront of NEUVE CHAPPELLE received.	BETHUNE. Coubrichent Sqw 16.
	11		C & D Coys and Batt Headquarters inspected by C.O. Court Martial in R.E. Sapper held at Batt Hd Qrs. Press of which Major Walker and Capt Allfree were President and Member respectively.	
	12		Practice with gas helmets and inspection by Medical Officer. All leave stopped by Brigade.	
	13		Orders from Brigade to recall all ranks from leave by 18th inst. Orders for move received. Lieut H.J. Jones rejoined from leave.	
	14		Battn left HINGETTE at 8.25.a.m. and marched to ESTAIRES where it arrived at 12 noon. Billeted in ESTAIRES for the night. A draft from England, 37 strong, arrived. Orders for move to trenches received.	
	15		C.O. Adjt. O.C. Coys, Bombing & Sniping officers visited trenches in the morning. Battn Relieved 17th Royal Scots (Bantams) in the trenches in the FAUQISSART Section. Battn in the RIGHT SUBSECTOR. 10 & S.W.B. in LEFT SUBSECTOR. Relief Complete by 10 p.m. Capt Mellor rejoined from leave. Casualties 1 killed & 4 wounded.	

WAR DIARY
or
INTELLIGENCE SUMMARY
(Erase heading not required.)

Army Form C. 2118

Place	Date	Hour	Summary of Events and Information	Remarks and references to Appendices
FAUQISSART	16th		Batt^n in the trenches. Capt Sheriff Roberts wounded.	
	17th		Batt^n in the trenches. Capt C.H. Jones rejoined from leave.	
	18th		Batt^n in the trenches. Officers of 16th Welsh regt visited the line to make arrangements re relief on 19th. Casualties 1 O.R. killed.	
FAUQISSART & LAVENTIE	19th		Batt^n in trenches. Relieved in the evening by 16th Welsh Regt. A well carried out relief completed at 9.30 p.m. Batt^n moved into support at LAVENTIE. "C" Coy found posts in supporting point behind the lines.	
	20th		Batt^n at LAVENTIE, general clean up of arms and billets. Inspection of arms and accoutrements, clothing &c.	
	21st		Batt^n at LAVENTIE, general clean up of arms and billets. Casualties 10, Rank killed while on fatigue duty. "Good Friday" Church services held.	
	22nd		Batt^n at billets both during morning, large parties found for wiring and strengthening defensive positions. Easter Sunday. Church services in billets.	
	23rd		Coy^s & O.Ralls mounted. Relieved 16th Welsh in trenches in the evening. Relief complete 9.05 p.m.	

Place	Date	Hour	Summary of Events and Information	Remarks and references to Appendices
FAUQUISSART	24th		In trenches. Casualties 3 O, Ranks wounded. 2nd Lieuts Williams, White and Vanderplank joined from England.	
	25th		In the trenches. Draft of 52 O, Ranks arrived from England and were posted to Coys.	
	26th		In the trenches. The C/Sgt Flower & one of his officers of 13th R.W.F. visited the lines. Casualties 6 O,R wounded.	
LAVENTIE	27th		Relieved by 16th Welsh Regt. Relief complete by 9.30 p.m. Battn marched to billets in LAVENTIE. Gas alarm and down the line from Aubrehame on the LEFT caused "Support" troops to stand to arms for an hour. Alarm false, all returned in. "B" Coy in supporting posts.	
	28th		In billets. Day spent in cleaning up & inspection etc.	
	29th		In billets. Orders for move received. The Sgts held a concert in the evening.	
	30th		Battn relieved by 13th Battn R.W.Fus. & marched at 12 noon to billets in Brigade Reserve area near MERVILLE. A hot day which caused the men. Battn in billets by 4 p.m. at ROBERMITZ.	Sheet 36A K 2 & 4 d.

WAR DIARY
or
INTELLIGENCE SUMMARY
(Erase heading not required.)

Army Form C. 2118

17 Rly widet Inf
Vol 6
XXVIII

8/71
6.0.
10 sheets

Place	Date	Hour	Summary of Events and Information	Remarks and references to Appendices
ROBERMETZ	MAY 1st		Battalion in training. Practice with gas helmets, time tests etc. Capt Oliver proceeded on leave.	P.W.
	2nd		Inspection of billets and Transport by Brigadier. He expressed satisfaction with all he saw.	P.W.
	3rd		Battalion marched to Forest of NIEPPE for musketry training. The change was much appreciated by all ranks.	P.W.
	4th		Tactical scheme for all officers in the Battn. N.C.O's & men at close order drill under Regtl Sgt Major.	P.W.
	5th		Baths at LA GORGUE allotted to the Battalion. The baths have a capacity of 100 men per hour. A clean change of underclothing is given to each man on quitting the tub. The soiled clothing being sent to the laundry. These baths are a convenient institution and are always thoroughly appreciated by the N.C.O's & men.	P.W.
	6th		Battn allotted the rifle range at LE SART (near forest of NIEPPE). Musketry instruction very actively resumed in the Battn. Plenty of keenness for improvement. Inter Battn Sports with 10th S.W. Borderers took place in the afternoon in which the latter Regt won all the prizes.	
	7th			

WAR DIARY
or
INTELLIGENCE SUMMARY

(Erase heading not required.)

Army Form C. 2118

Place	Date	Hour	Summary of Events and Information	Remarks and references to Appendices
ROBERMITZ	MAY 7th		Church parade in fields. All religions catered for during the day. 2/Lieuts Jenkins & Shinglecton reported for duty from the O.T.C. at St OMER.	P.W.
	8th		C.O., O.C. Coys, M.Gun Officer & others visited the new sector in the lines whilst a rear party took over the relief next day. Battⁿ in training in billets.	P.W.
	9th		Battⁿ marched off at 2 pm, after a very pleasant stay in billets, to take up new position. The embussed occupied by the battⁿ on January 14th in the cow shed over the day (Battⁿ H.Q. situated in a dilapidated mass of brick called EBENEZER farm) a place of many and fearsome odours, dead rats and decayed sandbags, being the most predominant. Regiment on LEFT Subsector — 10th S.W.B. Regiment relieved, 18th Lancs Fusiliers 35th Division (Sanitary)	P.W.
	10th		Battⁿ in trenches in MOATED GRANGE Sector. Casualties: 1 O.Rank wounded.	P.W.
	11th		Battⁿ in trenches. 1 O.rank Killed 3 O.ranks wounded.	P.W.

WAR DIARY or INTELLIGENCE SUMMARY

Army Form C. 2118

Place	Date	Hour	Summary of Events and Information	Remarks and references to Appendices
TRENCHES MOATED GRANGE Section.	12th		Batt⟨n⟩ in trenches. Casualties 2 O. ranks killed 2 O. ranks wounded. Relief Orders received.	P.W.
	13th		Batt⟨n⟩ in trenches. About 1.30 a.m. enemy sprung a small mine near our line causing the following casualties to a returning patrol :- 2/Lieut White wounded, 10 O. Ranks killed, 10 O. ranks missing, 15 O. ranks wounded & suffering from shock. Men behaved well under trying circumstances. Batt⟨n⟩ relieved in the evening by 16th Welch. Relief completed by 10.30 p.m., Batt⟨n⟩ marched to support billets at RIEZ BAILLEUL.	P.W. ☆ BETHUNE continued shelled.
RIEZ BAILLEUL	14th		Batt⟨n⟩ in billets. Church parades. Baths stopped at PONT RIQUEUL.	P.W.
	15th		Batt⟨n⟩ in billets. Reinforcements — 17 O. ranks — arrived from England.	— do — P.W.
	16th		Batt⟨n⟩ in billets. Parades and gas drills. Musketry exercises etc. N.C.O.s at Musketry instruction under Adjutant and Sgt Major, improvement shewn & much willingness to learn.	P.W.
	17th		Relieved 16th Welch Regt in trenches. Good relief, no casualties.	P.W.

WAR DIARY
or
INTELLIGENCE SUMMARY
(Erase heading not required.)

Army Form C. 2118

Place	Date	Hour	Summary of Events and Information	Remarks and references to Appendices
	May 18th		Batt'n in trenches. 3 O. ranks wounded.	P.W.
	19th		Batt'n in trenches. During the afternoon an enemy rifle grenade unluckily fell near "A" Coy. H.Q. dugout and did considerable damage to the occupants. Capt C.H. Jones (Comg "A" Cy), Frank Cathrall, J.R. Jones and Stark all wounded, the 2 first named, rather badly. 3 o ranks wounded.	P.W.
	20th		Batt'n in trenches. 2/Lieut Williams wounded, also 2/Lieut T.O. Thomas. Coy 2.M.S. H.Q. proceeded on leave to U.K.	P.W.
	21st		Batt'n in trenches. 2/Lieut Williams died of wounds. C.O. proceeded on leave. 1 o. rank killed 6 o ranks wounded. Batt'n relieved in the evening by 16th Welsh Reg't after a rather unfortunate tour in the trenches. Relief completed by 10.30 pm. Marched to billets at RIEZ BAILLEUL, MERVILLE.	P.W.
	22nd		Batt'n in billets. Funeral of 2/Lt Williams Batt'n at gun practice, Musketry instruction etc.	P.W.

WAR DIARY
or
INTELLIGENCE SUMMARY

Army Form C. 2118

Place	Date	Hour	Summary of Events and Information	Remarks and references to Appendices
REIZ BAILLEUL	23rd May		Battalion in support billets. Inspection of arms, gas helmets, equipment & clothing. Fatigue parties found for R.E. Bathing.	P.W.
	24th		In billets. Musketry exercises in small parties under cover. Lectures on a new method of adjusting gas helmets. 3rd A.S. Edwards proceeded on leave to U.K. 2/Lieut Parry and J.R. Jones rejoined from leave.	P.W.
ROBERMETZ	25th		Batt'n left REIZ BAILLEUL at 10.30am and marched to ROBERMETZ there to be in Divisional reserve. Relieved by 16th Bn R.W.F. (113th Bde)	P.W. X Near MERVILLE Sheet 36A.
	26th		In billets. Bathing at baths in MERVILLE. Training in walking and running, musketry exercises, attack practice etc.	P.W.
	27th		In billets. Tactical scheme for officers under Major Walker.	P.W.
	28th		FOREST OF NIEPPE. Battalion at close order drill. (Sunday) Church parade in the open.	P.W.

Army Form C. 2118

WAR DIARY
or
INTELLIGENCE SUMMARY
(Erase heading not required.)

Instructions regarding War Diaries and Intelligence Summaries are contained in F.S. Regs., Part II. and the Staff Manual respectively. Title Pages will be prepared in manuscript.

Place	Date	Hour	Summary of Events and Information	Remarks and references to Appendices
ROBERMETZ	29th May.		In billets. Roads reconnoitred to facilitate movements to reinforce any portion of the 11th Corps front. Billeting party proceeded to an area nearer the line to select the ground and move on the event of an enemy attack. Training carried on. Concertina wire made with a view to putting firing line in a better state of defence.	P.W.
	30th May.		Heavy artillery action commenced about 8 p.m. and continued with great violence for 3 hours. Brigade "Stood to arms", 2 battalions, the 16th Welsh Regt & 11th S.W. Borderers took up their forward and approach rendezvous. Bn's were not required to move. "Stand down" was received at 10.40 p.m.	P.W.
	31st May.		Battalions in training. Large fatigue parties found to work with R.E in making further tunnels for protection of units. The disturbance of the previous night was due to a report that the enemy were attacking. Presently the whole artillery demonstration made him taken the consternation.	P.W.

H.J. Walker Major

1875 Wt. W 593/826 1,000,000 4/15 J.B.C. & A. A.D.S.S./Forms/C. 2118.

WAR DIARY or INTELLIGENCE SUMMARY

Army Form C. 2118

17 R.W.F.

June

Place	Date	Hour	Summary of Events and Information	Remarks and references to Appendices
ROBERMETZ	JUNE 1st		Battalion in billets. Training and R.E. working parties found.	P.W.
	2nd		In billets. Training.	P.W.
	3rd		In billets. Route march carried out.	P.W.
	4th		In billets. Sunday. Church service held. The C.O. & Coy. Comdrs. visited the trenches at FAUQISSART to familiarise selves on the 5th.	P.W.
FAUQISSART	5th		Batt^n. left billets at 4 p.m. and marched via LAVENTIE to the trenches in the RIGHT Subsector of FAUQISSART. Relief completed at 10.30 p.m. H.Q^rs. and "C" Coy 2/4 Ox. v. Bucks L.I. attached for instruction.	*Laventie BETHUNE COMBINED Sheet.
	6th		In the trenches. Cas^ties. 1 O.R. wounded.	P.W.
	7th		In the trenches. A good piece of work was performed by the batt^n. in conjunction with the 10th S.W.B^rs. on our LEFT, in digging a trench on "No mans Land" across a large re-entrant. The work was cut through before dawn and linked up to old trench by a communication trench. No casualties were occurred throughout the operation which was a success. Gas attack was reported on our LEFT which proved false.	P.W.

7 G^l 9 sheets

WAR DIARY
or
INTELLIGENCE SUMMARY
(Erase heading not required.)

Army Form C. 2118

Instructions regarding War Diaries and Intelligence Summaries are contained in F. S. Regs., Part II. and the Staff Manual respectively. Title Pages will be prepared in manuscript.

Place	Date	Hour	Summary of Events and Information	Remarks and references to Appendices
FAUQISSART	JUNE 8th		In the trenches. The Coy of 2/4 Oxon & Bucks L.I. were relieved by a company of the 2/4 "The Bucks". Both of these units are Territorials. The Platoons in general, officers & men decidedly keen on getting information and of increasing their efficiency.	P.W.
	9th		In trenches. Relief Orders received.	P.W.
	10th		Relief commenced at 6 a.m. Batt: relieved by 2/1st Bucks. As the relief took place in daylight, it was of long duration, having to be done in very small parties of men. Bucks Bn entered in twos & threes & distances. The Batt: formed up near LAVENTIE and at 2pm marched to billets at ROBERMETZ.	P.W.
ROBERMETZ	11th		Batt: marched to billets at ROBECQ, the whole of the 38th Welsh Division being on the move South, destination unknown.	P.W.
ROBECQ	12th		In billets at ROBECQ. Inspection of Arms, clothing equipment, iron rations etc. 2/hour Exam. given in staining ammunition.	P.W.
	13th		Memorial services held for the late Lord Kitchener - impressive. Billeting parties went South to AUCHEL *	P.W.
AUCHEL	14th		Marched to AUCHEL (about 10 miles) troops marching well. Found time first forward 1 hour at 11am. A big mining district had currently going likely.	Sent 5A. P.W.

1875 Wt. W593/826 1,000,000 4/15 J.B.C. & A. A.D.S.S/Forms/C. 2118.

WAR DIARY
or
INTELLIGENCE SUMMARY
(Erase heading not required.)

Army Form C. 2118

Instructions regarding War Diaries and Intelligence Summaries are contained in F.S. Regs., Part II. and the Staff Manual respectively. Title Pages will be prepared in manuscript.

Place	Date	Hour	Summary of Events and Information	Remarks and references to Appendices
AUCHEL	JUNE 15th		Marched to CHELERS* (14 miles) Troops in good marching trim & shewing good spirit. A big difference in the country on arrival. South, a hilly country partaking the place of the flat country of FLANDERS. The billets about approached by all ranks. C.O returned from leave.	*LENS sheet.
CHELERS	16th		Battalion in billets, ready to commence Divisional training in "Open Warfare". Coys dug & prepared British & German lines of trenches.	P.W.
	17th		Training commenced (on ground about 2 miles N. of CHELERS) with Coy training, and advance of Bayonet fighting, Musketry, rapid loading etc., Gas helmet practice, fire control. Sweated shirt etc. Training lasts 5 hours in the ground. Dinner in the open.	P.W.
	18th		Church Services (Sunday) convened by the Brigadier & all officers & N.C.O's.	P.W.
	19th		Coy training on Manoeuvre ground.	P.W.

1875 Wt. W593/826 1,000,000 4/15 J.B.C. & A. A.D.S.S./Forms/C. 2118.

WAR DIARY
or
INTELLIGENCE SUMMARY
(Erase heading not required.)

Army Form C. 2118

Place	Date	Hour	Summary of Events and Information	Remarks and references to Appendices
CHELERS	JUNE 20th		Coy training in trenches seen. Coys showing marked improvement. Attacks on imaginary position carried out; all ranks showing a keenness to make things as realistic as possible and working well.	P.W.
	21st		Coy training as per programme shewn in "Appendices".	I. Programme shewing nature of work in "Coy" training. P.W.
	22nd		Batt⁺ in training. Batt⁺ practised in the attack.	P.W.
	23rd		Batt⁺ in training as per attached "Operation Orders".	P.W. II. Operation Orders for an attack.
	24th		Batt⁺ in training. "Artillery formation" practised also extending to avoid loss from rifle fire.	P.W.
	25th		Divisional field day in which all ranks worked well. The period 19th to 20th was productive of good results. Many items of training were brought home to the men that they had not seen before, and they shewed a marked improvement daily. A very satisfactory week's work ended and the men being very efficient, keen and fit.	P.W.

WAR DIARY
or
INTELLIGENCE SUMMARY
(Erase heading not required.)

Army Form C. 2118

Place	Date	Hour	Summary of Events and Information	Remarks and references to Appendices
CHELERS	JUNE 26th		No parade until the evening. At 5¼ P.M. Batt⁵ marched for NEUVILLETTE (S.W. of CHELERS 16 miles). A fairly long march performed in almost tropical rain. Men in good marching trim. Arrived 1.15. a.m. Y men were billeted in killed with good dry straw.	LENS Sheet. P.W.
NEUVILLETTE	27th		Marched to LONGUEVILLETTE (about 8 miles). Men marching much better than other march in the Division. Arrived 1. a.m.	P.W.
LONGUEVILLETTE	28th		Orders received for march on TOUTENCOURT (15 miles) received, but cancelled later. Batt⁵ rested for day & night. Remained in billets.	P.W.
	29th		March to TOUTENCOURT cancelled for the day.	P.W.
	30th		Marched to TOUTEN COURT at 3. p.m. Owing to motor column halted about 4 miles from destination from 8 to 10 p.m. Arrived in billets at 12.15 a.m. Batt⁵ marched well.	P.W.

J.W. Boland Lt.Col.

115th Inf.Bde.
38th Div.

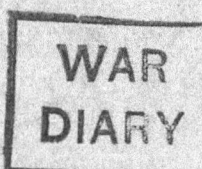
WAR DIARY

17th BATTN. THE ROYAL WELCH FUSILIERS.

J U L Y

1 9 1 6

Attached:

Appendices.

Army Form C. 2118

WAR DIARY
or
INTELLIGENCE SUMMARY
(Erase heading not required.)

Instructions regarding War Diaries and Intelligence Summaries are contained in F.S. Regs., Part II. and the Staff Manual respectively. Title Pages will be prepared in manuscript.

Place	Date July	Hour	Summary of Events and Information	Remarks and references to Appendices
TOUTENCOURT	1ST		Battalion marched from TOUTENCOURT to ACHEUX at 9.30 PM arriving ACHEUX 12 outskirts of midnight and BIVOUACED. 115TH BDE remained ACHEUX over night.	LENS 11
ACHEUX	2ND		Battalion BIVOUACED. BRIGADE ORDERED that men should rest as much as possible	LENS 11
	3RD		Battalion BIVOUACED. BATTALION left for BUIRE at 6.15 PM arriving BUIRE at 10 AM where BILLETED	AMIENS 17 + SHEET 62D NE TRENCH MAP
BUIRE	4TH		BATTALION BILLETED. Resting and awaiting further orders.	SHEET 57D NE TRENCH MAP
	5TH		BRIGADE orders UNITS to be prepared to move any moment. ORDERS received to move off at NOON. BATTALION Fell in and moved off at 1 PM for FRICOURT which village was captured by the 1ST R.W.F. on July 1st. BATTALION halted in a valley about 1/2 ML E of MAMETZ VILLAGE. Transport moved in ECHELON formation and was halted at point about 5 mile from the line. Rations waggons on cookers from here to the Battalion which travelled through FRICOURT E arriving at their destination about 3.30 am on the morning of the 6th.	

1875 Wt. W593/826 1,000,000 4/15 J.B.C. & A. A.D.S.S./Forms/C. 2118.

WAR DIARY
or
INTELLIGENCE SUMMARY

Army Form C. 2118

Place	Date	Hour	Summary of Events and Information	Remarks and references to Appendices
MAMETZ	6TH		Battalion under orders to proceed to the LINE. Congratulatory message received from MAJ-GEN SIR IVOR PHILIPPS Cmdg 38th Division just before Battalion left. The Message was read to all ranks. Battalion left for trenches at 2:30 p.m. B Coy occupying LINE MONTAUBAN ALLEY (S26c 1.1 & S27 b 10.9) about 1100X NE MAMETZ VILLAGE. "C D & A Coys in support in trench immediately in rear. Bn HQ being at the TRIANGLE" H8 c9 1.4. B Coy relieved by Coy of 113TH BDE during the evening. Casualties 3 O.R. Killed & 30 R wounded.	57D M.E SMITH
	7TH		BATTALION moved up to the attack upon MAMETZ WOOD. BDE attacked at 8 a.m. the 10th Battalion Welsh Regiment leading. Our Battalion in reserve. BRIGADE suffered rather heavy Casualties during the day, but ours were slight. Casualties 4 OR Killed 7 OR wounded. 2/Lt ROWE + 10 R wounded at duty. The Battalion was due the be relieved this night and withdrew from the ATTACK. H + C Coys & 1/2 MG Section were however left in the 2/NE	
	8TH		1/2 BN clearing up unpleasant equipment etc as the weather conditions in trood/MZE has been stubbornly bad. Remainder of Battalion due to be relieved by 114th Bde in the evening. Casualties 10 OR wounded.	

WAR DIARY
or
INTELLIGENCE SUMMARY
(Erase heading not required.)

Army Form C. 2118

Place	Date	Hour	Summary of Events and Information	Remarks and references to Appendices
	9th		A & B Coy H2MG Section went into billets on the 8th as expected, but returned to tents at about 3pm on this day. Battalion awaits orders in the evening again. Casualties 1OR killed 2OR wounded. Orders to rest until early morning received.	
	10th		At midnight on the 9th D Coy two orders to proceed to POZIERES REDOUBT to report at HQ 114th Bde for purpose of carrying ammunition up to the FRONT LINE. REVEILLE for remainder of Battalion at 2am. Battalion ready to march off at 3am but received orders until about 8am when the Battalion marched off to QUEEN'S NULLAH to support the 113th BDE who were attacking MAMETZ WOOD from the S. The Battalion was placed at the disposal of the G.O.C. 113th BDE. At about 12:30 pm the Battalion was moved up in Artillery formation from QUEEN'S NULLAH over the RIDGE and entered the South Easterly edge of the WOOD — A Coy entering on the left of the main drive running from the WOOD from SE to NW — B Coy entering in the centre & on the right of the main drive — and C Coy on the extreme right with their right flank in touch with the 10th Welsh 114th BDE. On the edge of the WOOD the Battalion was extended into LINE and advances in that formation through the WOOD which had already been cleared by the 113th BDE. to the Drive running from X 24a2.6 to 19a3.2.	

WAR DIARY or INTELLIGENCE SUMMARY

Army Form C. 2118

Place	Date	Hour	Summary of Events and Information	Remarks and references to Appendices
	10TH (CONT'D)		Battalion arrived at the DRIVE at about 7.30 pm and then fought their way forward with magnificent spirit as far as the 2nd line running from X19.d.10.2 to S19.a.8.8 when they arrived at about 8.30 pm. The 13th Welsh moved on our right and the 38th R.W.F. was on our left. The G.O.C. 113th Bde ordered that the general advance to the edge of the wood would take place at 4 p.m. This advance was carried out and the Battalion got within 30 x of the edge of the wood by about 6.30 p.m. when they immediately started to dig themselves in. Patrols which were pushed forward nearly to the edge of the WOOD reported the young wounded (?) instinct clear of the enemy. It was so mentioned that a definite clearing of the wood out soldly by the centre of the wood and its complete occupation was carried out sadly by the 14th R.W.F. Several Officers bear testimony to the splendid behaviour and conduct of our men and to the brilliant and determined way in which they succeeded to advance in spite of the density of the undergrowth. During the latter part of the advance some of our men in their tremendous eagerness to get to close quarters with the enemy pushed so far forward that they headed into our BARRAGE. Between 600 & 70 prisoners were taken in the course of the afternoon. The Commanding Officer and SIX Subalterns were wounded during the attack. After taking their position for a short time the Battalion pushed to the edge (N.W.?) of the wood dug themselves in about 250 x from the edge of the WOOD and relieved in this position over night, pushing ARTILLERY on the NORTHERN part of the wood and relieved in this position over night, pushing patrols well out in front.	

WAR DIARY or INTELLIGENCE SUMMARY

Army Form C. 2118

Place	Date	Hour	Summary of Events and Information	Remarks and references to Appendices
	10TH		About mid-night 2 Officers were killed. The Officers left track in RESERVE went for and arrived in the WOOD at about 3am, and subsequently the Adjutant left suffering from shell shock. Total casualties OR during day about 150 killed & wounded.	
	11TH		Early next morning of the 11TH the various Battalions reorganised and on completion we held the centre of the WOOD from the main drive to the Railway. The 11th SCOTS being on the right and the 10th Welsh on our left. At noon orders were received from the General for the advance to the bushes forward of the WOOD. Attack to commence at 3oClock. Message however received at 2.15 pm from the General to the effect that the attack was postponed until 3.30 pm. Battalion at 3.30 pm went forward to the attack & was in action until relieved early on the morning of the 12TH. We sustained further casualties in Officers & suffered very heavily in OR. Officers killed 3, wounded 4. OR killed 30 wounded 197. Accidentally wounded 1 Missing 37. RANK attached 1 OR wounded. Names of Officers killed during whole period of action at Mametz — Capt A Williams, 2/Lt Sinnett Jones, 2/Lt W.R. Wright, 2/Lt A. Lewis. Names of Officers wounded, Lt Col Ballard, Capt Strange, Pindleton, 2/Lt J R Jones, 2/Lt R Jones, 2/Lt D.J. Kunkler, 2/Lt HE Van Denham R, 2/Lt JW Walsh, 2/Lt C Gale, P.J. Rumpler, 2/Lt HE Van Denham R, 2/Lt JW Walsh, 2/Lt C Gale, 2/Lt E Thomas, Lt A Edwards, Lt A Styles. Capt C Walker RAMC Bn MO	

WAR DIARY or INTELLIGENCE SUMMARY

(Erase heading not required.)

Army Form C. 2118

Place	Date	Hour	Summary of Events and Information	Remarks and references to Appendices
	12TH		Battalion relieved from the LINE early in the morning by the 4TH DIV IN and returned to Bivouac. Orders for Battalion to be ready to move off at any time after 2 pm received. Transport left at 4 pm. Single ration per Railway journey. 10.7 pm orders received to delay move until 5 am following day.	
	13TH		Battalion moved off to WARLOY; TRAIN arrangs cancelled. Arrived WARLOY about 1.30 pm. Orders received to stand fast & be prepared to move off immediately by BUSES to COLIN. Battalion moved off at 7 pm. Settled down for night in BIVOUAC at COLIN.	
COLIN 14TH			CO Adjt & Capt Seagh YMG left for Bde HQRS by 11 am. CO Adjt & GOC VIII Corps inspected Battalion in the BIVOUAC lines at 1 pm. GOC VIII Corps inspected Battalion moved off at 2 pm to BIVOUAC in MARCHING ORDER. Battalion moved off at 2 pm to BIVOUAC at COIGNEUX.	LENS SHEET 11
COIGNEUX 15TH	16TH		Battalion remained in BIVOUAC. Day devoted to clean up of Battalion at rest. Bathing during morning. Battalion at D.H.Q musketry firing — CO Adjt & Corps Sig Offr & MGO left to inspt. THE NORTH. S. Relief orders for 18th received.	LENS SHEET 11

WAR DIARY
or
INTELLIGENCE SUMMARY
(Erase heading not required.)

Army Form C. 2118

Place	Date	Hour	Summary of Events and Information	Remarks and references to Appendices
	18TH		Battalion prepare to move off at 2p.m. to relieve the 16th Welsh in the trenches. At 7p.m. relief completed but for one Platoon which could not be relieved by daylight. Lt Col D Grant-Dalton reported at HQRS but did not go to the trenches. Casualties 1 Officer 9 OR wounded. Officer wounded 2/Lt Singleton.	SHEETS 57 NE TRENCH MAP
	19TH		Battalion in trenches. Lt Col D Grant-Dalton joins for duty with the Battalion. Casualties 10 R wounded.	
	20TH		Battalion in trenches. Casualties 1 OR wounded	
	21ST		Battalion in trenches. Relief orders received. Casualties 1 OR wounded	
	22ND		Battalion relieved from the trenches during afternoon by the 16th Welch. Casualties 1 OR 1 Killed + 1 OR wounded. Battalion in Billets at COURCELLES	
COURCELLES	23RD		Battalion in BILLETS. Voluntary Church Service held. Battalion employed on fatigue work pushing in front LINE TRENCHES.	TRENCH MAP 57 NE

WAR DIARY or INTELLIGENCE SUMMARY

Army Form C. 2118

Place	Date	Hour	Summary of Events and Information	Remarks and references to Appendices
	24th		Battalion in BILLETS — Bathing at COUIN during morning. Employed on fatigue + working parties during afternoon + evening in front line trenches.	
	25th		Bn in BILLETS — Battalion employed on fatigue work late day + night in the TRENCHES. Inspection of arms, ammunition, clothing, equipment + gas helmets. Casualties NIL. Relief orders received.	
	26th		Relieved 16th Welch in the trenches. Relief complete at 9 pm. Engaged in consolidating OLD BRITISH FRONT LINE in AUTHUILLE WOOD & bit known by name of the "BATH". Casualties NIL.	
	27th		Battalion in trenches. Consolidating FRONT LINE + WIRING. Relief orders received. Casualties 3 OR killed	
	28th		Battalion in trenches. Casualties NIL. Officers of both Bdes inspect the line preparatory to taking over. 6/8 Edwards reported for duty as 2nd in command.	
	29th		Battalion relieved by 10th Battalion — KSLI commencing at 9am. Complete at about 12.45pm. 6.30 am. Battalion march out by platoons to COURCELLES where they assembled to march off for billets in BUS. Battalion arrived in BUS at 4pm. Afternoon devoted to foot + kit inspections.	
	30th		Battalion billeting party left at 4 am for St Omer.	

Army Form C. 2118

WAR DIARY
or
INTELLIGENCE SUMMARY
(Erase heading not required.)

Instructions regarding War Diaries and Intelligence Summaries are contained in F. S. Regs., Part II. and the Staff Manual respectively. Title Pages will be prepared in manuscript.

Place	Date	Hour	Summary of Events and Information	Remarks and references to Appendices
	30th		Your Battalion left BUS en route for CANDAS. Battalion halted at Grecourt (Sheet 57d) in Bivouac. Voluntary Nonconformed service on the way.	KENS 11
	31st	12.6 am	Regt Transport left Bivouac for CANDAS STATION.	
		1.30 pm	Battalion marched off for CANDAS STATION.	
			Battalion entrained at CANDAS and left for ST OMER arriving there about 11.10 am.	HAZEBROUCK 5a
			Battalion marched from ST OMER to Billets at WATTEN.	

J B Cockburn Lt Colonel
Comm^{dg} 17th R. W. Fus^{rs}

APPENDICES.

SPECIAL ORDER OF THE DAY

by

MAJOR GENERAL IVOR PHILIPPS, D.S.O.

Commanding 38th (Welsh) Division.

Wednesday, 5th July, 1916.

To,
THE OFFICERS, N.C.O's AND MEN OF THE 38th (WELSH) DIVISION.

You have worked hard for many months with an energy and zeal beyond praise to fit yourselves for the task you have voluntarily undertaken. You have undergone the hardships of a winter campaign with fortitude. You have earned the praise of your Corps Commanders for your courage, discipline and devotion to duty. You have now held for six months a section of the British line in France, during which time you have not allowed one of the enemy to enter your trenches except as a prisoner, and on several occasions you have entered the enemy's lines. 11 Officers and 44 N.C.O's and men have already received rewards from the King for gallant and distinguished conduct in the field. Your fellow countrymen at home are following your career with interest and admiration. I always believed that a really Welsh Division would be second to none. You have more than justified that belief. I feel that whatever the future may have in store for us I can rely upon you, because you have already given ample proof of your worth. During the short period in the Training Area you worked hard to qualify yourselves for still further efforts. I thank you most sincerely for the loyal and wholehearted way in which you have all supported me and for the way in which each one of you has done his utmost to carry out the task allotted to him. With such a spirit animating all ranks we can one and all look forward with confidence to the future, whatever it may have in store for us.

You are to-day relieving the 7th Division, which has attacked and captured German trenches on a front of a little less than one mile and for a depth of about 1¼ miles. In this attack the village of Mametz was captured, the enemy have suffered very heavy casualties, 1,500 German officers and men were taken prisoners and six field guns were captured.

The 1st Battalion, Royal Welsh Fusiliers and the 1st Battalion. Welsh Regiment of the 7th Division have both distinguished themselves in this attack, and I am confident that the young battalions of the famous Welsh regiments serving in the 38th (Welsh) Division will maintain the high standard for valour for which all three Welsh Regiments have been renowned throughout the war.

To be read to every Platoon and Section on parade.

Ivor Philipps
Commanding 38th (Welsh) Division.

Weekly Duty State for week ending July 2nd 1916
17th Battalion Royal Welsh Fusiliers

Distribution		Offrs	W.O	NCO	Men	Totals
Available for Duty.		22	4	60	578	664
Hospital		4	2	2	34	42
Coy Employ:-	Cooks			1	16	17.
	Stretcher Bearers				15	15
	Q.M.S. + Storemen.			4	4	8
	Officers Servants				21.	21.
	Signallers				8	8
	Runners				6	6.
	Sanitary + Scavengers				19.	19.
	Snipers				1	4	5.
Regimental Employ:-						
	Officers	6				6
	R.S.M.		1.			1.
	M.G. Section			4	47	51.
	Signallers			3	18	21.
	Transport.			3	41	44
	Runners			1	9.	10.
	M.O's Employ.				3	3.
	Postman			1		1.
	Police			2	2	4
	Orderly Room.			2	1	3.
	Q.M. Stores		1	2	4	7.
	Shoemakers			1	2	3
	Sanitary				1	1
	Officers Servts.				10.	10
	Pioneers			1	2	3
	Cooks				2	2
	Stretcher Bearer				1.	1
On Command, Brigade Employ. etc I.B.D.		3		7	64	74.
	Totals	35	8	95	912	1050

Weekly Duty State for Week ending July 9th 1916.
17th Battalion Royal Welsh Fusiliers

Distribution		Offrs	W.O.	NCO	Men	Total
Available for Duty.		23	3	62	549	637.
Hospital		7	2	2	32	43.
Company Employ :-	Cooks			2	15	17.
	Q.M.S. & Storemen			4	4	8
	Signallers				8	8
	Runners				5	5
	Sanitary, Scavengers & Pioneers				19	19.
	Stretcher Bearers				15	15
	Servants & Grooms				25	25
Regimental Employ.	Officers	5.				5
	R.S.M.		1.			1
	M.G. Section			5	43	48
	Transport			3	41	44
	Signallers			3	20	23
	Runners			1	8	9.
	Q.M. Stores		1	2	4	7
	Servants & Grooms				10	10
	Shoemakers			1	2	3.
	Cooks			1	2	3
	M.O.				3	3
	Pioneers			1	1	2.
	Orderly Room			2	1	3
	Police			1	4	5
	Postman				1	1
	Sanitary				1	1
Brigade Employ, Command, IBD etc.,		2		8	88	98.
Totals		37	7	99	900	1043.

Weekly Duty State for Week ending July 16th 1916.
17th Battalion Royal Welsh Fusiliers

Distribution		Offrs	WOs	NCO	Men	Total
Available for Duty.		8	2	34	319	363.
Hospital.		7	2	2	30	41.
Company Employ:	Cooks			2	13	15
	Stretcher-Bearers				13	13
	Signallers				6	6
	Servants				9	9.
Sanitary, Scavengers & Pioneers					12	12
Q.M.S. & Storemen				4	4	8
Runners					4	4
Regimental Employ:—	Officers	4				4
	R.S.M.		1.			1.
	M.G. Section			4	32	36
	Signallers			2	18	20.
	Transport.			2	44	46
	Runners				8	8
	Q.M. Stores.		1	2	4	7
	Servants				7	7
	M.O.				1	1
	Orderly Room.			2	1	3.
	Postman				1	1
	Police			1	3	4
	Pioneers			1	2	3.
	Sanitary				1	1
	Cooks			1	1	2
	Shoemakers			1	1	2
Brigade Employ, Command, IBD etc.		2		14	107	123.
	Casualties	17	2	25	267	311.
	Total.	38	8	98	374	1051.

Weekly Duty State for Week ending July 23rd 1916.
17th Battalion Royal Welsh Fusiliers

Distribution	Offrs	W.O	NCO	Men	Total
Available for Duty	9	3	53	253	31
Hospital	6	2	4	40	52
Company Employ:— Cooks			2	16	18
Servants				11	11
Stretcher-Bearers				16	16
Sanitary, Scavengers & Pioneers				16	16
Q.M.S & Storemen			3	4	7
Signallers & Runners				14	14
Snipers			1	4	5
Grooms				2	2
Regimental Employ:— Officers	5				5
M.G. Section			8	32	40
Transport			3	43	46
R.S.M.		1			1
Signallers			2	16	18
Postman				1	1
Orderly Room			2	1	3
Q.M. Stores			3	5	8
M.O.				3	3
Cooks				2	2
Pioneers				2	2
Runners			1	17	18
Servants				6	6
Police			1	3	4
Shoemakers			1	2	3
Grooms				2	2
Brigade Employ, Command I.B.D. etc.			1	10	116	127
Casualties	14	2	21	246	283
Totals	35	8	115	867	1025

Weekly Duty State for Week ending 30th July 1916.
17th Battalion Royal Welsh Fusiliers

Distribution	Off'rs	W.O's	N.C.O	Men	Total
Available for Duty	10	4	49	239	302
Hospital	5	1	4	32	42
Company Employ:- Cooks			2	16	18
Stretcher bearers				16	16
Signallers				9	9
Servants				14	14
Runners				10	10
Q.M. Sts & Storemen			4	4	8
Pioneers, Sanitary & Scavengers				20	20
Snipers				4	4
Regimental Employ:- Officers	6				6
R.S.M.		1			1
Machine Gun Section			5	46	51
Signallers			2	18	20
Transport	1		3	42	46
Runners			1	18	19
Q.M. Stores		1	2	4	7
M.O's Employ				3	3
Orderly Room			2	1	3
Pioneers			1	4	5
Cooks				2	2
Servants				5	5
Postman				1	1
Police			1	3	4
Grooms				3	3
Shoemakers			2	2	4
Brigade Employ, Command, I.B.D. etc.	3		9	102	114
Casualties	3	1	14	127	145
Totals	28	8	101	745	882

Army Form C. 2118

17 R.W.F.

WAR DIARY or **INTELLIGENCE SUMMARY**
(Erase heading not required.)

August 1916

Place	Date	Hour	Summary of Events and Information	Remarks and references to Appendices
WATTEN near ST OMER	Aug 1 1916		Batts: in billets. Inspection of arms, clothing and equipment by Coys. App A. General cleaning up. Beautiful weather	App A
	Aug 2		Batt: in billets. Inspection in field marching order by Commanding Officer. Medical Inspection. Swimming parade in the afternoon. (Signal) Divisional Orders received stating that 26223 Sgt T. Hurt had been awarded the MILITARY MEDAL.	App B
VOLKERINGHOVE	Aug 3		Batt: left WATTEN at 4.30 pm to move up nearer the line, and arrived at VOLKERINGHOVE 6.30 am. Morning devoted to inspection and cleaning up generally - men resting in the afternoon.	App C
	4		Batt: in billets. Morning devoted to training in Physical Drill, Platoon & Coy Drill, and Musketry. In the afternoon - bathing parade and clothing drill. Officers and NCO's reconnoitered in Coy recruit and R.S.M - word of command and drill.	App D
	5		Batt: in training. Physical Drill, Platoon & Coy Drill, Musketry by Coy & Platoon commanders. Batt: inoculated against Para-Typhoid. 2nd half of officers NCO's & men for Special rewards submitted to Bde Office.	App E 9 G 16 Muck

WAR DIARY
or
INTELLIGENCE SUMMARY
(Erase heading not required.)

Army Form C. 2118

Place	Date	Hour	Summary of Events and Information	Remarks and references to Appendices
HOLLEBEKE NOVE	Aug 6 1916		Bath in Milch. Church Parade. Lecture after on "Esprit de Corps" new draft of 2 NCO's & 33 men - Welsh Regt - arrive from ARNEKE Sh.	See 9.
	7		Bath in Milch. Carrying on with training - Draft with and mules & Lewis C. Lehue arrived by Motor Lorry. Comsponder an important finish Lecture Survival for Officer.	
	8		New draft of 2 NCO's & 54 men arrive from 2/5 Royal Welsh Fusiliers. Batt. inspected by Brigadier General Commanding who on the whole was pleased with the Batt.	
	9		Batt in Milch - carrying on with the training - machine gun to lecture on gas and gas helmet practices. Several Officers away on leave.	
	10		Batt. shelled Batt. at ZEGGARS CAPPEL B.10.C. - marched to Bath by bgs - hacherels Advanced and rear Guards on the way. Lecture on Sanitation at 10th S.W.B. Headquarters by Divisional Sanitary Officer. Fine weather continues	

WAR DIARY or INTELLIGENCE SUMMARY

Army Form C. 2118.

(Erase heading not required.)

Place	Date	Hour	Summary of Events and Information	Remarks and references to Appendices
	1916			
OLKERINCKHOVE	August		Baths and training. See Appendix No 2 - Programme of work	No 2 Programme of work 11th to 13th
Sheet 27 BELGIUM	11		Batt. inspected at 11.30 am by Lieut Gen Sir Hubert Gough KCB Dso commanding VIIIth Corps. He inspected the general appearance and cleanliness of the men, fitting of the equipment, cookers, Bible Members, Officers', NCOs', Officers' Messes and Officers' Belongings. At conclusion the men by his wish attacked No. Several cases of eyes under age submitted to DAG. Base. Three days for consideration. 14 cases disposed of in the usual manner - under 18 sent down to Havre, under 19 moved to a training unit behind the firing line.	Ap. 2 Att Map
FRANCE G9R10	12		Baths and training - Co [traced?] for the afternoon. Officer No 2. Report by two Officers and Sketch of Reconnaissance asked for in attend No 14 entrusted to Brigade	Receive No X POPERINGHE
	13		Church parades - Parade as for programme of work appx No 2. Inspection of greatcoats by C.O. - a great many condemned. Very markedly infected. Bathing parade in the afternoon. The weather continues - Farmers busy with the corn.	Ap 4

WAR DIARY
or
INTELLIGENCE SUMMARY.
(Erase heading not required.)

Army Form C. 2118.

Place	Date	Hour	Summary of Events and Information	Remarks and references to Appendices
OLKERINGHOVE Sheet 27. BELGIUM & FRANCE G.9.d.10	Oct 14		Orders received from Division that the present system of instruction in Physical training, bayonet fighting, and Bombing is unsatisfactory and that in future, it should be organised by the Brigade and not by the Bn's. Offrs formed up on Training Area G.3.d.- instructors in the above on the subject right. Oct then carried out with the training of the Division was present.	App 1
	15		Both Training, Physical drill, Extended order, advanced stage, embracing fire discipline and fire control. Judging distances, feeling an important subject - by Gas & discipline etc - by Platoon / Coy commanders NCO's given to see the training that etc their men t wear the special chevron on the left arm as distinctive marks. Route march - 8am to 1pm. helping. Operation indication.	App 1
	16		Organisation and judging distances, Gas Shot. following in rear. Lecture at 3.30pm by Captain Betts, Aldershot, on Bayonet Fighting to the Commanding Offrs of Division & Bde Brigade. 4-6 pm Bombing and Bayonet fighting on Training Area.	App 1

WAR DIARY
or
INTELLIGENCE SUMMARY.

(Erase heading not required.)

Army Form C. 2118.

Place	Date	Hour	Summary of Events and Information	Remarks and references to Appendices
	1915			
OLKERINCKHOVE	Aug 17		Batt: training. Physical training, Extended Order drill, Gas helmet drill, bombing & Bayonet fighting. 2 Lt Cathcart attended gas in. on left sample as 2nd at 4 O. Reinforcements of 44 men arrived. Estimate of Chewing gum to troops. To keep the mouth and throat moist during hot weather — early to bed. Brigade.	Nex†
	18		A party of 6 men detailed to assist French farmers with the corn harvest. A few showers today after a long drought. Batt: training, Physical Exercises Extended Order drill Attack formations, Gas training and Bayonet fighting. Brigade School Exercise 60 and 4 Offrs. Attended at A.D.M.S. Survey inspected Battalion lines and billets. About 1 am on night of 18th/19th a message was received from Brigade, instructing C.O. & Corp. Signalling Officer to proceed to the trenches to inspect the line at 9am message received that Batt: was to entrain at BOLLEZEELE commencing at 9.40am Companies moved off at 8.40am. Transport team left at 10am Batt HeadQrs did not	Nex†
	19		leave until 1 ½ pm. Entrained at 3.30pm arrived in POPERINGHE	Nex†

WAR DIARY / INTELLIGENCE SUMMARY

Army Form C. 2118.

Place	Date	Hour	Summary of Events and Information	Remarks and references to Appendices
POPERINGHE	Aug 19 1916		About 8.15 pm halt rested for a few hours in the HOP FACTORY and entrained again at 10 pm, leaving 10.40 pm and arriving in YPRES (Asylum) about 12 midnight. Marched into billets. C & D Companies at Machine Gun Farm. Batt. Headquarters and A & B Companies on Canal Bank. Relieved the 2nd Batt. Lancashire Fusiliers. Btn Brigade Relief completed Batt. reliefs	# 5 Central Sheet 9 C.25 a.c. Sheet 28
YPRES	20		in billets at 1.40 am on the 20th. Gas pit and Quakeshaker Store # POPERINGHE. General cleaning up of clothing & Rifles and Gas Helmets to Inspection received from Bde. regarding the action to be taken in the event of "Gas Alert" or "Enemy Gas Attack" C.O. inspected the billets and dug-outs – boundary arrangements in this area for being complete and saho-factory. Apart from a few shower the day was fine, weather continues fine	
	21		Both in billets – Inspection parties for R.E.s at night. Lectures and Instructions by day. Wiring party under 3 P. Popham. At 8.30 pm Gas alarm was given by 146 Brigade. All men made with their	

WAR DIARY or INTELLIGENCE SUMMARY

Army Form C. 2118.

Place	Date	Hour	Summary of Events and Information	Remarks and references to Appendices
YPRES	1916 Aug 21		Gas helmets in fighting order. Alarm of a front 9.45 p.m. - No Blackor Artillery. Bombarded the enemy's front line for two hours during the afternoon - retaliation drew was slight but ineffective.	No 1
	22		Relief in full. 60 others. Cond of Enquiry at POPERINGHE.	App
	23		Wiring behind continued. 1 Officer (Lt Tp Horsfield) Journed wiring behind continued. Also 6 O.R. previously serving with the Bath wounded from Kimmel Park - also 6 O.R. previously serving with the Bath wounded and call on reinforcements Bath. relieved the 16 Welsh Regt in the trenches - relief commenced at 9pm - completed at 11.30pm - Major Cuthbert wounded in the knee who went up to the trenches. Disposition of the trenches - Bath Headquarters Junction of BOARS LANE and CONEY STREET L20 d 5.4 Sheet 28 NW. A - Right Coy - 3 Platoons in front line L21 a 8.8 - to MORTELDJE SAP 1 Platoon in ATLAS TR B - Left Coy - 2 Platoons in front line L 14 d 9.7½ to C14 d 5.6½ 2 Platoons in VICKER'S LANE C - Centre Coy - 2 Platoons in front line MORTELDJE SAP to C14 d 9.7½ 2 Pls at CLIFFORDS TOWERS. D - Support Coy in Bath Headquarters - less 1 Platoon in ATLAS TRENCH 29th Division relieved on the night of Bde. 11 Bde on our left.	No 1

WAR DIARY or INTELLIGENCE SUMMARY

Army Form C. 2118.

Place	Date	Hour	Summary of Events and Information	Remarks and references to Appendices
YPRES	1916 August			
	24		Batt. in the trenches – quiet all day - machine gun activity during night. Casualties:- 1 O.R. killed, 1 wounded. C.O. visits the line and makes arrangements for the one coy. in Reserve at BHQ to proceed to the WILLOWS in support to the "A" Coy. "A" Coy of the Left Reserve Batt. (16th Welch Regt) was moved up to take over the reserve position of Batt H.Qrs. Reliefs completed at about 11.30 pm. Major J. Parsons (The Welsh Regt) joined for temporary duty as 2nd in command vice Capt G.W Edwards wounded. 1 2nd Lt Price Welsh Non Com Chaplain left fm funnel park, and left "A" Williams M.C Chaplain arrived to be attached the Bn instead of him.	Ap. 27 Ap. 28 Ap. 29 App. 30
	25		Batt. in the trenches. Enemy very quiet all day. Casualties 0R 4 killed and 3 wounded – all K we shell the only shell put over during the afternoon, unluckily 6 s.m.	App. 30
	26		Batt. in the trenches. Wind S.W during the two days 1st Australian 1 I.O.R. who went out on patrol at 11 pm were	App. 30

WAR DIARY
or
INTELLIGENCE SUMMARY.

(Erase heading not required.)

Army Form C. 2118.

Place	Date	Hour	Summary of Events and Information	Remarks and references to Appendices
YPRES	1916 Aug 26		wounded on duty. Battalion in the trenches. Casualties NIL Relieved by the 16th Welsh Regt and Battalion - via "D" Coy which remained in Reserve at Brielen Headquarters 16th Welsh - moved out as follows - to "C" Companies to Canalbank A Coy to Moulin du Son Brigadier General Horatio Evans left for England. Brigadier General Marden took over the Brigade temporarily and inspected the Battalion here	Also It's Curnow
	27th		In the afternoon of the 27th Casualty Other ranks 1 wounded. Battalion - billets out move - made inspection and instruct Marched to Quartermaine. 2nd in Command and 2 other officers attended a Trench Mortar and Mine demonstration accompanied by Infantry assault at WISCQUES near ST OMER Win from Corps. — ROUMANIA has declared war on AUSTRIA. ITALY has declared war on GERMANY Major J Evans of 20th Rest. reports for duty — took command of "C" Coy Also Lieut H Morgan historians who	Also

Army Form C. 2118.

WAR DIARY
or
INTELLIGENCE SUMMARY.
(Erase heading not required.)

Place	Date	Hour	Summary of Events and Information	Remarks and references to Appendices
YPRES.	1916 Aug 28		who served previously with this Batt. and was wounded in the week. He took command of A Coy.	
	29		Batt. in billets - fatigues and lectures in the morning - ready in the afternoon - R.E. fatigue parties at night. Change in the weather. Raining all the morning. Batt. employed by night on R.E. work and General Defences. Six Officers reinforcements arrive. Major W. Evans posted to command "B" Coy. Lieut A. Morgan Williams posted to command A Coy. Others officers posted 3 to B Coy 2 to D Coy but 1 to A Coy.	App
	30		Batt. in billets - relieving afternoon with morning inspections & lectures. Continued wet and bad weather. Heavy night work. Relief orders received.	App 1
	31		Batt. in billets ready to proceed. Relief orders issued. Relieved 16th Welsh Regt in the trenches subsector. Relief complete at 17/30 a.m.	App 1

J. B. Cockburn Lieut Col.
Commanding 17th Batt. R.W.F.

Army Form C. 2118

WAR DIARY
or
INTELLIGENCE SUMMARY
(Erase heading not required.)

Instructions regarding War Diaries and Intelligence Summaries are contained in F. S. Regs., Part II. and the Staff Manual respectively. Title Pages will be prepared in manuscript.

Place	Date	Hour	Summary of Events and Information	Remarks and references to Appendices
YPRES	Sept 19th		Bath in the trenches. G.O.C. Brigade inspected the line in the morning and G.O.C. Division in the afternoon. Enemy shelled our front line – T.20 & T.21 – also BOARS LANE Communication trench in the afternoon about 3–4 pm.	Apx D
		2	G.O.C. 114th Brigade and 2 C.O.'s from same Bde. visited the line.	Apx A
		3	Two "Gas alarms" in the early morning – had reliefs on for nearly an hour – no gas attack. Relieved by the 15th Welsh Regt and marched to Machine Gun Farm.	
		4	Battalion arrived at Machine Gun Farm. Inspection carried out.	
		5	Battalion in Reserve. Orders for relief received. Battalion relieved the 14th R.W.F. in Right Right Left Divisional Sector. H.Q. THOIX TOUR CHATEAU. While relief was being carried out the 14th Welsh Regt. 114 Bde. took up Left Reserve position in the Right sector. Relief was complete by midnight. On relief 14th R.W.F. move off as G. Divisional Reserve.	Apx B

WAR DIARY
or
INTELLIGENCE SUMMARY.
(Erase heading not required.)

Army Form C. 2118.

Place	Date	Hour	Summary of Events and Information	Remarks and references to Appendices
YPRES	19/2/16		Relief orders issued and published. The C.O. inspected Bt.C. Coys. and Bn. H.Q. Battalion commenced to relieve the 13th Bde. R.W.F. 113 Bde. at 8 p.m. Right Coy. relief completed at 3 a.m. 7 inst. during this time the 16th R.W.F. Regt. was relieving the 16th Welch. Centre Regt. in Left Sub sect Right Sector on relief the 16th Welch was taking up the left sector. Right Reserve Batn. H.Q. TROISTOUR CHATEAU. The 13th R.W.F. on relief were taking up the supporting points until the 16th Welch were available. After which time the 16th Welch Regt. Coys. D Coy. outposts line points 2 and 13th Battn. R.W.F. moved up to supporting 2nd Sub's. I.n. matto. H.E.K. intgon and H.Q.O. left for service at Divisional school. Relief complete at 3 a.m. Wind horrible so heavy gun attack throughout the day. Germans found us bring it during the afternoon. Shot 8 p.m. "Jand" Feis and Watoto worst heavily Bombard. Fire ceased down to lm/inic but only few casualties. All quiet again at about 11.30 p.m.	YPR YPR

WAR DIARY
or
INTELLIGENCE SUMMARY.
(Erase heading not required.)

Army Form C. 2118.

Place	Date	Hour	Summary of Events and Information	Remarks and references to Appendices
YPRES	1916 Feb 8		Battn. in trenches during the early hours of the morning a German patrol party was caught in the wire and 2 of them who were on one of the posts who taught our	9oR
		9	Batts. in junction. Artillery shelled enemy transports in moving about 4 bn. at C.13 & 8½ q. Our dug outs in machine gun but out of action.	9oR
		10	Relief orders received and published. Relief commenced at 2pm. Reliefs commenced at noon O & D Coys. Relieved and relief by 2 Coys of 10" Welch. Remaining 2 Coys. and Battn. H.Q. relieved in the evening.	9oR
		11	Relief complete and Batts. in new area 1.15am (Calvados). Breakfast at 8. Bay details to inspection. Int's interview to Bn. Col. C Galliance took R-B Battn.	9oR
		12	An 2 Lieut P. Rose to report for duty with battalion. Battalion employed in fatigue work. Batt. H.Welch Hostel Strady our Battalion.	9oR
		13	Battalion employed as fatigue work. Batt. Welch. 2/Lt Arena 9/R Duke 9oR	9oR

WAR DIARY
or
INTELLIGENCE SUMMARY.
(Erase heading not required.)

Army Form C. 2118.

Place	Date	Hour	Summary of Events and Information	Remarks and references to Appendices
YPRES	Sept 19		Battalion in hutts. Brigade in terminal Reveille. Notice received that Corps commander was likely to visit the camp during the day but he did not appear. Men employed cleaning up the camp.	S.R.
	20		Battalion in hutts. Men on parade till 12.30 pm. Afternoon hot and slept. Paths of 200 men & officers employed on fatigue work from 7 pm. to 1.30 am. 2nd Army Commander passed through the camp during the morning.	S.R.
	21		Battalion in hutts. Shall Box Respirators issued to the Battalion. Company commanders received instructions in the method of (non salient) inspecting officer arranged a testing chamber to test the fitting which the respirator had all men too breath through it and had their respirators finally fitted the eye being noted in the instruction of each them pay been 6 hour an spray 4 officers and 200 men for night fatigue party — Lendewarde Battalion in hutts. Men stated in the morning. In the afternoon	S.R. S.R.
	22			

WAR DIARY
or
INTELLIGENCE SUMMARY.

Army Form C. 2118.

Place	Date	Hour	Summary of Events and Information	Remarks and references to Appendices
YPRES	1916 Sept 13		Normal country between H.2 and canal. Battn in billets. Relief order received. Move tomorrow to trenches.	
	14		March from hospital. Relief 16th Batt. establish in trenches commencing at 2 p.m. C2 two relieving by day and B by night. Relief complete by 11.45 p.m. Cas. this off. Wilson (right) wounded. 22 O.R. 3 wounded. Too much MG fire for H.Q. Battalion in trenches. Intermittent enemy bombardment.	JPR
	15			Continues JR
			Battalion in trenches. Intermittent enemy bombardment. At 3 am and 7 pm, 11-8 pm to 12.30 am. Two casualties.	JPR
	16		Battalion in trenches. Relief order received.	JPR
	17		Battalion in trenches. Relief 14th Batt published. 14th R.I.R. commences relieving at 4 pm. 2 Coys relieved by day, 2 Coys after dark. Relief complete by 12 pm. Casualties nil. D Coy. to 3 tn. 18th Sept. Two runners not return later. 3 tn. 18th Sept.	J.P.R.
	18		A week in camp about 5 am. 18th Sept. Battalion in billets. 3 men reported absent 2 of them returned during the day. One remained absent.	JPR

WAR DIARY or INTELLIGENCE SUMMARY

Army Form C. 2118.

Place	Date	Hour	Summary of Events and Information	Remarks and references to Appendices
YPRES	Sept 22		The Battalion together with two other Battalions of the Brigade were inspected by General Sir Herbert C.O. Plumer G.O.M.G. K.C.B. Commanding Second Army. 4 officers and 200 men on night fatigue party.	9 P.R.
	23		Battalion in billets. Morning on parade. Platoons, Coys and Bn respirator drill. Lecture and bayonet fighting. Afternoon. Rest and sleep. 4 officers and 200 men on rifle grenade party. Court martial convened on Pte. [?] of [?] promulgated.	9 P.R.
	24		Battalion in billets. Sunday church service. Commanding Officer attended. Instruction Rousing Parties on Bailout Zionder. After bath on night work.	9 P.R.
	25		Battalion in billets. Order to commence officer's day classes to physical drill. Bayonet fighting and rifle training party on light work. Eventually ordered to strike Camp. 2 officers bombardiers School [?] forthwith to B[?]	9 P.R.

WAR DIARY or INTELLIGENCE SUMMARY

Army Form C. 2118.

Place	Date	Hour	Summary of Events and Information	Remarks and references to Appendices
YPRES	Feb 26		Battalion 8/2 O.R. & 4 Myroland proceeded on both Relief order received. Raiding party under instruction of Lyt. Sergt. B. for fired 6 Lange Charge. 5th Tpmey 5th Rehr 2nd with her Explosive.	9.P.R.
	27		10W. under Company Armaments. Orders received delaying relief for 24 hours. Relief Orders issued.	9.P.R.
	28		Battalion in Billets. Battn. Parade at 10 AM. Promulgation of orders of G.O.C. Court Martial on Pte Griffiths punishment Apparitia. Strength of Bn. 6 Officers & Pte. # Rank 1217. Numbers listed as members. Relief commenced at 2 p.m. Battn left Camp D for Canal Bank relieving the Right reserve Battn. on the Right Dr. Sector (10-2010) 4.65. relief the Coy of Support Batt. at Help Right from Battn IRISH FARM H.Q. & movement of companies on CANAL BANK. Relief upon completed at 11.30 p.m. Battn. HQ attached to 114 Brigade temporarily.	9.P.R.
	29		Commanding officer, 9/c Companies, Lewis Gun officer, Bombing officer and Signalling officer tour the line held by Rest. Front Battn relieving HQ 9 am. Relief due to commence after 12 midnight owing to shelling of noorchee.	9.P.R.

WAR DIARY
or
INTELLIGENCE SUMMARY.
(Erase heading not required.)

Army Form C. 2118.

Place	Date	Hour	Summary of Events and Information	Remarks and references to Appendices
YPRES.	Oct 1 29		Relief delayed owing to postponement of operation. Relief commenced at about 1.30 p.m. on 30 October and was completed at 6.15 p.m. Battalions attacked to 114 Brigade.	J.P.R.
	30	HQ IRISH FARM 2.40am	Battalions in trenches R.C. & B boys in the line (C.21.7 & C.22.1) & Coy in support, and arrival at a.follows. 4 Pat. Line Posts. S.14.d & S.16.b messages post consisting of 6.1 Off & 2 Officers. Remainder IRISH FARM 19 Off. 1 mon and FRESCATI 1 Off. 20 men + 2 Platoons (40 men) of 13th Welsh Rgt. IRISH FARM army command of the Hqy 17 R.W.F. acting as Support. Quiet day. Inquired by air burst shelling by both sides about 8.30 p.m. A fighting patrol of 2 officers + 18 O.R. went out to CANADIAN DUGOUTS found them empty. Hunk dangerous	J.P.R. J.P.R.

G R Powell Major
Comdg. 17 R. Welsh Fus.

WAR DIARY or INTELLIGENCE SUMMARY.

Army Form C. 2118.

17 R.W.F. Vol II

Place	Date	Hour	Summary of Events and Information	Remarks and references to Appendices
YPRES	1916 Oct 1		Battalion in trenches. A patrol of 2 officers and 8 O.R. set out at 10am. to reconnoitre CANADIAN DUGOUTS. They found the place unoccupied. Casualties for the day 1 O.R.	9pk
	2		Battalion in the trenches. Day quiet. At 8am a raiding party of 2 officers and 8 O.R. went out with the object of killing any Germans or capturing prisoners for the purposes of identification. They found the Dugouts strongly manned and thus impaired upon endeavouring no casualty — extended. When jackets in their house.	9pk
	3		Battalion in trenches. Day quiet, none except relief operations. Relief commenced at 7pm. Battalion relieved 11th South Staffs Relief completed about midnight. The 15th Brigade took over the sector 9pk, R.W.F. division. Or Relief the Battalion moved into Brigade Reserve Left Subsector.	98
	4		Battalion in Brigade Reserve. H.Q. & 1 Coy attached to Sintram 2 Coys Hospital Bank and one Coy at Left front Bn. Rightsector H.Q.	11G 10 huts

WAR DIARY
or
INTELLIGENCE SUMMARY.
(Erase heading not required.)

Army Form C. 2118.

Place	Date	Hour	Summary of Events and Information	Remarks and references to Appendices
YPRES.	1916 Oct 4		The day devoted to Inspection and cleaning up. Fatigue parties to R. Engineers comprised of all available men supplied	J.R.
	5		Battalion in Brigade Reserve. Inspection under company arrangements carried out in the morning, the men resting and cleaning in the afternoon. Battalion's employed at night on fatigue work. Quartermaster's party (Cyclists at B. Reserve B. Band etc.	J.R.
			left in the afternoon.	
	6		Battalion in Brigade Reserve. Inspection in the morning. Rest in the afternoon and fatigue parties at night.	J.R.
	7		Battalion in Brigade Reserve. Inspection in the morning. Rest in the afternoon, and fatigue parties at night. Orders received delaying	4.2.20
			the relief which was to have taken place this night. Relief	J.R.
			offer Jan Lohey	
	8		Batt. in Bde Reserve. Men employed in cleaning up and on fatigue. Relief commenced as soon as light permitted and was completed	J.R.
			by 10.30 p.m.	

WAR DIARY or INTELLIGENCE SUMMARY

Army Form C. 2118.

Place	Date	Hour	Summary of Events and Information	Remarks and references to Appendices
YPRES	1916 9/10		LEFT SUBSECTOR. RIGHT SECTOR. Battalion in trenches. Bangaluh went out to reconnoitre for raiding party and further patrol work. The raid to be carried out on CAMPIDIAN DUGOUTS. The party left our line at about 5.30 pm. The visibility being high on account of the moon they were evidently observed by the enemy shortly after starting, as the party which divided into two small parties as it approached the dugouts found them $ strongly manned and surrounded by front wire. The outer party got into position but the burning cartridge - most especially being on the right - was seen who! The enemy seeing known here and the party had to retire receiving heavy machine gun fire. Casualties: 2 officers wounded, 3 OR wounded and 1 OR counted missing. A search party of 1 off. 48 OR however failed to find the missing man. Battn in trenches. Enquiry being heavy battn went out to avoid no man's land - Battalion Hdqrs. Reconnoitering patrols sent out to NEWTEDGE STRT but failed to obtain information owing to strong light enemy	

WAR DIARY
or
INTELLIGENCE SUMMARY.
(Erase heading not required.)

Army Form C. 2118.

Place	Date	Hour	Summary of Events and Information	Remarks and references to Appendices
YPRES.	1916 Oct. 11.		Battalion in trenches. Day quiet. No casualties owing to active reconnoitring. Patrol went out but failed to obtain information. Patrol reports that the Battn. could be relieved that night at 10.30 a.m. Relief commenced at 6.30 p.m. Battn. in billets by 11 p.m. HQ & 1 Coy. inclure Guntram, 2 Coy. Canal Bank & 1 Coy. in support to Left Front Battalion's Grande Reconnoitring Patrol of 2 Officers & NCO, 1 OR. went out to examine the Enemy wire at C.15. c.53.93 and Sap 18 and found it to be in a fairly strong good condition.	I.O.R.
	12.		Battn. in billets. Commanding Officer attended a two day course addressed by Bde. Commander. Men dust in cleaning up.	I.O.R.
	13.		Battn. in billets. Day devoted to inspections and dispong of stores to launding baths.	I.O.R.
	14.		Battn. in billets. Reliefs hours and published. Day spent by Bn'ls inspections and diggers. Bn. commenced reliving the Battn. R.I.F. at 5.30 p.m. moving from Left Subsect Battn. RIGHT Ly Battn. R.I.F. at 5.30 p.m. moving from Left Subsect Battn. RIGHT SECTOR to Right Subsect'n. LEFT SECTOR. Relief reported complete @ 12 midnt.	I.O.R.

WAR DIARY or INTELLIGENCE SUMMARY

Army Form C. 2118.

Place	Date	Hour	Summary of Events and Information	Remarks and references to Appendices
YPRES	1916 Oct 14		2 Cos & 1 Coy at Chateau Trois Tours and two and a half companies in General Reserve the remaining half platoon being at Lancashire Farm Raiding Party left at Bachine Farm.	Appx.
	15		Battalion in trenches awaiting relief order received and published. Relief commenced at about 5.30 p.m. and was completed by about 9 p.m. 2 Battn. took over the Right sub-sector LEFT SECTOR. The disposition being 4 Coy on the right, C Coy in the centre and 5 Coy on the left. D Coy in support at LANCASHIRE FARM. The stay of B Coy & D Coy was uneventful between the other Coys. 2 platoons of the 16 Worcs. Regt. with one offr. who was detached between them arrived to the support of W. Coy. Rest of C.S. Coy remained there which companies while the taking of A & B Coys remaining on ORDINARY Coy was occupied on the ORDH DEFENCES. My hand quietly and loyal help.	
	16		Battalion trenches. Each day trenches in a bad state Drainage work was taken in hand all along the line. EATING TRENCH henceforth	

WAR DIARY
or
INTELLIGENCE SUMMARY.
(Erase heading not required.)

Army Form C. 2118.

Instructions regarding War Diaries and Intelligence Summaries are contained in F. S. Regs., Part II. and the Staff Manual respectively. Title pages will be prepared in manuscript.

Place	Date	Hour	Summary of Events and Information	Remarks and references to Appendices
YPRES	1916 Oct 16		Moved in in two places early am but to avoid breaks the enemy. The 16th Welsh brought another such attempt of 2 officers and 60 O.R. which assisted the R.E. in the construction of new trench and 2 P.R. the thickening of the parapets. Fighting Patrol under Lieut. Statham patrolled NO MANS LAND but did not encounter any hostile patrols. No casualties.	
	17		Battalion in the line. Day quiet. Both engaged as above with the 16th Welsh. Our trench above so D.I.H. shew on right of during the night. Bath Batt acted on but did not encounter any of the enemy. 2 P.R. 1 NCO + 16 O.R. taken out of the line and attached to the raiding party at MACHINE GUN FARM. Casualties Nil. Parties engaged with others as aforementioned	
	18		Battalion in the line. Day quiet but at night definite line was selected. Retaliation was asked for and given as which to 2 P.R. enemy classed line. Casualties Nil. Parties engaged as works as aforementioned. Battalion in the line. Day quiet. About 9 pm even new lot	
	19		of shell was that the trenches were obtaining owing to the heavy J.P.R. rains of previous days. We be our own and be together with	

WAR DIARY or INTELLIGENCE SUMMARY

Army Form C. 2118.

Place	Date	Hour	Summary of Events and Information	Remarks and references to Appendices
YPRES	1916 Oct 19		The working party from 16 Welch Regt. were improving Dark Lake to north and the flanks and communication trenches. The quantity of which are at first rather numerous will enhance to the minimum. A lighting patrol which went out did not meet any of the enemy. It reported that the wire along our front was in a weak state and that the German wire to the North of ION HUCKS COTTAGE was strong. The patrol also came across hostile take Louws from our wire trenches to about between the centre and left companies towards the German wire. The Hearing of the front line be strong, both unsuccessful with Bataillon NW.	JPR
	20		Battalion in trenches. Day quiet. Relief orders received and Battalion relieved by the 16th Welch Regt. Relief complete at about 9pm. The information received in the battle the evening right was handed over to the incoming units. Battn. marched out and Coys of the support billets at the CANAL BANK — 2 Companies and 1 Coy, and the two drafts at the Chateau 3 Oles Inns.	JPR H.B.W.

T2134. Wt. W708—776. 50000. 4/15. Sir J. C. & S.

Army Form C. 2118.

WAR DIARY
or
INTELLIGENCE SUMMARY.
(Erase heading not required.)

Place	Date	Hour	Summary of Events and Information	Remarks and references to Appendices
YPRES	1916 Oct 21		Battalion in billets. Day devoted to cleaning up. A party of 2 officers and 30 men assisted the R.E. on the duckwalks in Northern	J.P.R.
	22		half sub-sector LEFT SECTOR. Battalion in Hospe billets. Inspection of Arms, Equipment and feet etc. carried out. Church Parade service held by C of E. reverend midday. Some working party as a known night provided.	J.P.R.
	23		Battalion in Hospe billets. Prophasband Band were inspected. Two platoons proceeded to ELVERDINGHE CHATEAU to bathing. Inter a/Coy tournaments had been's training. Working party as a known night as yesterday.	J.P.R.
	24		Battalion in Hospe billets. Inspection and drill carried out. Relief orders received and issued. Relief commenced at 5.30 for the 13 Bdge? taking at the trench area. Relief complete and Battalion	J.P.R.
	25		in Camp D. arrived Battn. by 10 pm. Battalion in Camp D. Day devoted to cleaning but arms inspection of arms equipment.	J.P.R.

T/134. Wt. W708—776. 500 000. 4/15. Sir J.C. & S.

Army Form C. 2118.

WAR DIARY
or
INTELLIGENCE SUMMARY.
(Erase heading not required.)

Instructions regarding War Diaries and Intelligence Summaries are contained in F. S. Regs., Part II. and the Staff Manual respectively. Title pages will be prepared in manuscript.

Place	Date	Hour	Summary of Events and Information	Remarks and references to Appendices
YPRES	1916 26.26		Parade in camp D. Battn. attended Church; all those of Jewish faith on the 23rd inst. attended Parades including French instructor, close order drill and Bayonet fighting. 4 Reinforcements of 2 Officers and 160 joined for work on wiring cable.	92R
	27		Battalion in camp D. drills in the morning. the new draft being under special escort of NCO's. hot and fine afternoon and fatigue parties of 2 offs and 100 ors as usual.	92R
	28		Battalion in Camp D. drills in the morning. the new draft continuing and reinforcement training. hot on the afternoon and also a party of 2 offrs and 160 ors at night. It learn received at 11.30am. Battalion stand up or march on the alarm and to be ready to move. The Battalion was ready to move off at 12.15 pm. Transport horses all in etc ready loading complete by 1.50pm. The Brigadier General commanding was present and he inspected the Battalion.	92R
	29		Battalion in Camp D. Uniform parade in the morning or dress of C.Church Parade. — Coy. E. encampment drill X.6. Fatigue Party.	92R

WAR DIARY or INTELLIGENCE SUMMARY

Army Form C. 2118.

Place	Date	Hour	Summary of Events and Information	Remarks and references to Appendices
YPRES	1916 10.30 30		of 3 officers and 200 O.R. proceeded at night. Battalion in bomb shelter in the morning & right receiving second training. Rest in the afternoon and fatigue party of 3 officers and 150 O.R. trench at night.	QR
	31		Battalion in bomb shelters in the morning & rest afternoon with the progressive training. Rest in the afternoon. Fatigue party of 4 officers and 200 men. Trenches at night. Lieut Colonel Gault Bart, stg. Major, Durham L.I. Comdg. 6 Royal Irish Regt. assumed command of the Battalion. Major E.H. Powell left for England.	QR

H J Taylor Colonel
Comdg 17 R.B.E.

WAR DIARY
or
INTELLIGENCE SUMMARY
(Erase heading not required.)

Army Form C. 2118.

1/ R.W.F.

Vol 12

12 G.
12 sheets

Place	Date	Hour	Summary of Events and Information	Remarks and references to Appendices
YPRES.	19.6		Battalion in Camp D. Parades under Coy. arrangements. Fatigues by night. R.B. Voluntary service 2nd in Col. Robinson M.J. Taylor reported for duty. Signal and v.ac. K. O.C. Capt. Thurston left Lewis Gun house (O.C. corp course) at 5.50pm. 2/Lt. Kilmington rejoined from Lewis Gun Course.	
	10.7		Battalion in Camp D. Parades under Coy. arrangements. Fatigues by night. 2/Lt. ... R.E. service all Sabbath. E.O.B. rec. all off of 16 to listen to RM? v... board at 12.15pm and address the officers on organisation of Labour... Later Lieut. Rowe rejoined from leave. Lieut. K.Evans rejoined from Lewis Gun School Le Touquet.	
	11.13		Battalion in Camp D. Parades under Coy. arrangements. Fatigues by night. ... ... visited the line. ...-ordin ... published. Chaplain the Williams He ... from hospital and R.W. - A.P. Hughes from Injury Course. Battn in Camp D. Batln. Blackadder 1961 working in the memory	

T2134. Wt. W708—776. 50C000. 4/15. Sir J. C. & S.

WAR DIARY
or
INTELLIGENCE SUMMARY.
(Erase heading not required.)

Army Form C. 2118.

Place	Date	Hour	Summary of Events and Information	Remarks and references to Appendices
YPRES	1916		and in clearing the camp in the afternoon. Broke at 11 pm	
			let the trenches. Marched to BRANDHOEK STATION. Entrained for	
			YPRES ASYLUM. Relieved the 15 Welsh Regt. Relief completed	
			at 10.10 pm. Dispositions B. Coy. in FRONT LINE, D Coy in	
			support at THE WILLOWS. A Coy. & 1 Platoon B. Coy in reserve at	
			Bn. H.Q.– RLY. LT. BELLE ALLIANCE. 2 Ltn. M. Ontario M'Lenegan	
			Reverted to base D.BATTLERS.	
	5		Battn. in trenches. Quiet day. Casualties Nil. Lightning patrol	
			went out to No MAN'S COT and Sap 18 about 70× W of it. 2Lt. Knowles	
			in command. 2Lt. I.L. Roberts accompanied them. The Saps are	
			spent to be unoccupied and no battle could be heard working.	
	6		Battn. in the line. Quiet day. Casualties Nil. A party of B Coy	
			100 yds or even in front of Right Coy., and a party of B Coy	
			under Lt. A. Coy. under Lieut. Leive Lt. Hughes took out a fighting	
			patrol to No M'S C battle encountered and no enemy patrols found.	
	7		Battn. in the line. Casualties Nil. Day quiet. Lt. Westmacott	

WAR DIARY or INTELLIGENCE SUMMARY

Army Form C. 2118.

Place	Date	Hour	Summary of Events and Information	Remarks and references to Appendices
YPRES	1916			
	7		Took out a fighting patrol to enemy barricade encountered parties engaged in whole fronts in putting out wire. The enemy of course aware, leading from the left of Bbay to the B.trench. Did not succeed. Shots.	
	8		Batt. on defence. Quiet. Bn walkin NW. I fired at Estanie. Took out a fighting patrol for second time tonight but did not encounter any enemy patrols. It was too wet and and. The enemy expected earth. About 9pm. a working party was about at HIGH COMMAND REDOUBT. Our artillery was informed and shortly on fire well. Relay over wire. C.O. at Bn conference at 11.30am. Lieut. Donovan joined us from 8 to 18/11/16.	
	9		Batt. in the line. The enemy shelled CODEY STREET in the afternoon. Our artillery retaliated on HIGH COMMAND REDOUBT. Chewalkin NIL. Bn. of prev. covered at 6pm. commenced about 5.30pm. Helbatt. Regt. taking over the same dispositions. It batt.	

WAR DIARY or INTELLIGENCE SUMMARY

Army Form C. 2118.

Place	Date	Hour	Summary of Events and Information	Remarks and references to Appendices
YPRES	1916 Nov 9		Upon being relieved moved into the LEFT RESERVE AREA. The distribution being thus: 1 Coy at Batt HQ. LEFT FRONT BATTN. 2 Coys on CANAL BANK EAST and Batt H.Q. and 1 Coy on CANAL BANK WEST. Capt G.R. Shingleton rejoined from Base on return to Tongres.	
		10	2 Lieut. Malcolm<?> joined reported from there. Battn in support. Day devoted to inspections under Coy arrangements. Party of 1 Officer + 13 OR's engaged in ENEMY DEFENCES – unearthing potatoes. 1 Officer + 70 OR on night fatigue.	
		11	Batts in support. Inspections. Party of 1 Officer + 70 OR's 10am to 12 noon + 2-4 pm work on CANAL BANK improvements. Same party on CANAL DEFENCES and 1 Officer and 70 OR on night fatigue. 1 NCO + 15 OR worked on Rear Batt HQ from 9.30 am to 12 noon ended. R.E. supervision. 1 NCO + 20 OR reported to HQ 123 Field Coy RE. 2 Lieut W.A.S. Kinnothrie<?> rejoined from Brigade (R.E. Adm't Office). 2 Lieuts G.B. Castle, R.S. Baird-Hynes<?> from Divisional School, Esperano. R.P. Daniel + J.K. Dale rejoined from 2nd Army School. Capt. R.G. Daniel	

WAR DIARY or INTELLIGENCE SUMMARY

Army Form C. 2118.

Place	Date	Hour	Summary of Events and Information	Remarks and references to Appendices
YPRES	1915 April 11		Left for Brigade – R.E. Intell. Officer Casualties. One Officer & Rank wounded.	
	12		Battn. in support. Sunday. Voluntary services in the morning. To work with on CANAL BANK improvements, proceeded with on the afternoon. Work on CANAL DEFENCES and RE. parties on redoubts etc. Jerque parties at night. Usual work recced.	
	13		Battn. in support. Inspection 9am to 10am. 10am to Noon and 2pm to 4pm. Work on CANAL DEFENCES. Work on CANAL BANK improvements. Work on CANAL DEFENCES & RE. parties as previous days. 2 Officers and 20 men on Regtl. fatigue.	
	14		Battn. in support. Inspection 9am to 10am. 10 to 12 noon work on CANAL BANK improvements. In the afternoon started to clear up billets. Battn. relieved by 1st Norfolk Regt., and relieved 1st R.W.F. in Right Route again. LEFT BRIGADE Disposition Battn. H.Q. & 1 Coy. TROIS TOURS CHATEAU. 1 Coy. CANAL BANK EAST. 2 platoons CANAL BANK WEST. 2 platoons LANCASHIRE FARM and 1 Coy. LA BRIQUE murmur.	

WAR DIARY
or
INTELLIGENCE SUMMARY.
(Erase heading not required.)

Army Form C. 2118.

Instructions regarding War Diaries and Intelligence Summaries are contained in F. S. Regs., Part II. and the Staff Manual respectively. Title pages will be prepared in manuscript.

Place	Date	Hour	Summary of Events and Information	Remarks and references to Appendices
YPRES	1916 Jan. 14 15		Lieut. R.O. Williams left the Batt^n for the Royal Flying Corps. Batt^n in Bgd Right Reserve Att^d Inspection and cleaning of equipment. Relief orders issued. Battalion moved to Right Front area and was disposed as follows. 3 Coys in Front Line and 1 Coy in support. 1 Coy of 16 Welch Bgd in Reserve in 6pth BMR Officers: O/c Riflemen RA Dennison O.W. left for Divisional School. 2/Lieuts. P. Williams and R. Sandys Jones joined Batt^n.	
	16		Batt. in the Line. Army to keep embarkment of enemy time opposite Batt. from Cog: to garrison of the Lake Bank Line, are mich trained in the support line never much. The enemy retaliation was weak. Lewis Mr. officer R.C. Bird took out a fighting patrol but did not encounter any hostile patrols. The enemy during the night was in a nervous condition and from a lasge number of very lights. 2/Lt. L.P.L. Davies left for Lewis Gun School. Lieut. Dent left on leave.	

Place	Date	Hour	Summary of Events and Information	Remarks and references to Appendices
YPRES	1916 Nov 17		Baboon shelters. The artillery bombarded the camp roads of the German line and today during the day. Further bombardment extension to 6.30pm + at 10.30pm to 11pm with a view to deceiving the enemy as to bomb where... was to be made. For the later bombardment a shoot turns & runs to High Command Redoubt which we thought raided. The garrison of which was again withdrawn for today. Retaliation was chiefly directed known CANTIN CITY. We were constantly subj. to enemy MMs. The work of building Dub. Elephant dugouts, drainage, and clearing of duckboards was proceeded with during the day. At night cops were sent out by the three Coys and the accumulators for the Coy. HQrs were increased. Bombardment on HIGH FOREST. A patrol was sent out in the early hours of the morning to ascertain if the enemy
	18		

WAR DIARY or INTELLIGENCE SUMMARY

Army Form C. 2118.

Place	Date	Hour	Summary of Events and Information	Remarks and references to Appendices
YPRES	1916 Mar. 17		Had any parties repairing the pumps & done to the front line. Enemy fired a few salvos short of front line. No mm's had to be put back.	
	18		Battalion in the line. Day comparatively quiet. Enemy this Mr. attacked we went out on the ground to keep a close contact on the German wire. Parties were observed & fresh wire and sandbags in evidence on the wire. Made notes of this and I sent on a copy to Brigade commanders for comment. They sent notes to the General commanding. Relief commenced. Capt O'Shaughn. returned from M. Corps School. Battalion on the line. Quiet. Tr. Brecu-Scio.	
	19		Relief commenced about 6 pm the 16th Welsh Regt. relieving. The Battalion when relieved moved to the left Rear area and were camped as follows. 3 Coy's Ent 2 Coy. TROIS TOURS CHATEAU. 1 Coy. BIVOUACS EAST and Macedon CAMP BIVOUACS WEST. HQ.N.S. while left at Perrach Wood. Mother Gertie & Pres. Sev. transport left at H.T. South. Saluting on Rosetta. Inspection under Bry department from of all Ranks up. Boots on Cmds. OFFICE S. taken. Only element the day working for woop in training.	

WAR DIARY or INTELLIGENCE SUMMARY

Army Form C. 2118.

Place	Date	Hour	Summary of Events and Information	Remarks and references to Appendices
YPRES	1916 Nov 20		and received reports on CANAL BANK. Battalion on fatigue. He went over to previous day's work.	
	21		Battalion on fatigue. Received reinforcement of 22 with Brigade H.Q.D.	
	22		Capt. Porter H.R. Nelson – C.O. & to report to Batt'n H.Q. Batt'n. Porter took fatigue at EVERDINGHE. Photographers of O.C. – attended the facts at EVERDINGHE. Photographers of M. attended the Coy. Capt. Morgan-Williams of No. an inspection day. Capt. Morgan-Williams by No. VIII Coy. Slow and sure but out the abdomen & C.Q.M.Sgt. his above. Casualties 1 O.R. wounded. Sergt. Jones and reported from C.a.t. Effect September. Returned from hospital	
	23		Battalion in fields. Inspection every Coy. arranged. Rifle oiled & ammunition made. The Regimental Padre medical officer delivered the on he some day. The medical officer delivered the officers and N.C.O's on the advice of Mont the one hr... in the tower en route to advise Dinah Nels my Smithson trans. Pres th'Oct granted leave pass... 3 of 6.	
	24		Battalion in fields. Inspection when Coy. arrangements.	

WAR DIARY or INTELLIGENCE SUMMARY

Army Form C. 2118.

Place	Date	Hour	Summary of Events and Information	Remarks and references to Appendices
YPRES	10/2 1922		Relief washed on miniature range. 2nd in command & the Coys. Lewis Gun Officer & C.O.s. (Lt/Adjutant) were on the 2nd IRISH FARM JCTBE preparatory to relief on 25/26 Officers & N.O.s arr. Hd. from Louis Bros & B.O.E.	
	25		Battalion in bivouac. Reinforcements received - Battalion relieved in ??? 18th R.S.F. by 6 p.m. ??? Relief of 18th Bn Argyll Rgt in Rigu Seen Rgt Bre (Irish Farm) - Relief of Companies (west to ?.C. completed 11/7 p.m. Suspicious. A. & D. Coy in reserve on R. line. R. Coy attached to each) in front line - R. Coy in reserve on ???. See W. Batt. H.Q. at IRISH FARM - 2/Lt E. R. Abraham ??? ??? Lock 46159 C. Coy reported missing.	
	26		Battalion in the line - Lieut. T. Davis and H.O.V. to Chepsline Divl. anti Bayonet fighting course 38th divisional school - 2.O.R. rejoined from leave - Casualties NIL. Cas. of ??? Koch reported on by 114 F. Recd. 2/Lt H. L. R. Morgan on patrol.	
	27		Battalion in the line. 1.O.R. to M.G. course at TERDIGHEM - 2 Officers and H.O.V. to M.G. course at 38 divisional School. 2/Lt H.S.R. Morgan and J. L. Williams. 2/Lt A.P. Hughes and S.O.R. moved on leave (two of them have been attached to R.E.s) Court of Enquiry into Pte Koch's case held by order of C.O. President Capt T. A. Styles.	

Place	Date	Hour	Summary of Events and Information	Remarks and references to Appendices
YPRES	1916 Nov 27		2/Lieuts 2/Lt A. Clarkson and J. A. Norris - Bitterers received. Capt Hughes (Staff Capt 114 Bn) now M.O. 3rd Welsh Regt. 2/Lt J. A. Norris on patrol - operation orders received from 114th Bde.	
	28		Battalion in the line. Casualties Nil. 2/Lt H.M. Jenkins on patrol - Warning received of intense bombardment of enemy lines opposite Ager Dim Fort - Orders issued to Companies accordingly. Bombardment progressed 2/hr home - Major Edwards, 2/hr Norris, 2/hr J. A. R., on patrol/reconnaissance in NO MAN'S LAND - which must battalion in the line - Major Edwards 2/Lt J.A. Stone and 1.0.R. on reconnoitring patrol during assault, taking advantage of dark mist Lt J. Mellor A Coy severely injured with a very pistol - Count of injuring him. Runner Capt W. G. Williams - Number Capt 9th Welsh C. F. 2/Lt J. A. Norris - orders for relief previous and published at noon. Bombardment 8 hrs to 9 hrs to opposite 55? to ensure front 9.45 p.m. Thru the Companies were not anyhow seriously. Battalion relieved by 13th Bn Welsh Regt, relief completed 10.p.m. Battalion entrained at YPRES ASYLUM at 2 a.m. and got into not billets (E CAMP P) at 3 a.m. Casualties on O.R. accidentally injured.	

WAR DIARY
or
INTELLIGENCE SUMMARY

Army Form C. 2118.

Place	Date	Hour	Summary of Events and Information	Remarks and references to Appendices
YPRES CAMP G. — Sheet 28 N.W. A16a 9,2	Nov 30		Battalion in rear billets. Inspection of Brigade by Corps Commander at Camp L at 2.15 p.m. The Corps Commander complimented the Battalion upon its smart appearance after 25 days in the line. 2/Lt Taylor St W. 17 R Welsh Fus.	

Army Form C. 2118.

WAR DIARY
or
INTELLIGENCE SUMMARY
(Erase heading not required.)

17 RWF

Vol 13

18 G.
12 sheets

Place	Date 1916	Hour	Summary of Events and Information	Remarks and references to Appendices
YPRES (near) CAMP G. Sheet 28 NW Alba.9.2.	1st		Battalion in rest Billets (Camp G.) — Battalion bathed at Camp D. Lt W.E. Notcutt struck off establishment. 2/Lts Morgan and T.G. Williams returned from Bois Carré.	
	2nd		Lt J. Lewis returned from P.T. and Bayonet fighting course. 2/Lt H.M. Jenkins and S.O.R. proceeded on leave. Regimental exercise to all officers and men under R.S.M. spade cleaning up, fitting up, of arms, clothing and equipment. Battalion employed in cable-burying at night. Fatigues: C Coy 2 gunca, B Coy 1 900d.	
	3rd		Sunday: Church Parades, C of E, R.C. and Nonconformist — 60 horses arrived. Physical training and scouting. Remainder of day resting in Ypres. Fatigues etc: A Coy 1 gun, D Coy 0. L N.C.O.'s to duties from Camp. Cable burying at night.	
	4th		2/Lt Davidson appointed Captain M.G. commanding a Company (formed 2/10/16). Bayonet fighting and Coy drill — Firing on range at L Camp. Course of Inginery into case of civilians seen in D Coy's lines — Arrangements of burial of Bandsman Lance-Corporal Lewis, Capt A.H. Williams C.F. in charge	

WAR DIARY or INTELLIGENCE SUMMARY

Army Form C. 2118.

Place	Date	Hour	Summary of Events and Information	Remarks and references to Appendices
G. CAMP.	Dec. 5th		A and B. Companies, Tactical exercise. Officers of C and D. See conduct under C.O. 2/Lt. A.J.T. Davis rejoined from his sick leave. 2/Lt A.H. Beal left to be instructor at Reinforcement Camp TROUEN.	
	6th		C and D Companies, Tactical Exercise. 2/Lt Potts Wadson left for Machine Gun Corps, Grantham. N.C.O.s Revue mustication course R.S.M. 2/Lt. I.Q. Roberts visits Battalion in left trenches. Rifle Brigade to make arrangements for their relief. Night fatigue, train to YPRES ASYLUM. Two Companies firing on range.	
	7th		Divisional Gas Officer instructs 2/Lt officers of no company. O.C.S. B and C Lits and R.M.O. visit the line to arrange relief details. Major Edwards and 6 o.r. proceed on leave. Trip on range. Allie arms inspected 8.20 a.m. Inspection of Leiw Respirators by 2/Lt W.E.R. Morgan - Chemist of Camp. Inspection of ambulances from ditto. 1/10th Kents came to CAMP.G. to life on site camp. Battalion left Camp at 8.40 p.m. to the railway near CAMP. E. and entrained for YPRES ASYLUM - marched by Platoons from ASYLUM	

WAR DIARY or INTELLIGENCE SUMMARY

Army Form C. 2118.

Place	Date	Hour	Summary of Events and Information	Remarks and references to Appendices
YPRES	Oct 8th (contd)		Arrived Gun Boots at Rendezvous E.Morinil and proceeded up CONEY ST. via LA BELLE ALLIANCE to the Left Sector Centre (Major Evison). Relief complete 9.6 p.m. Received W.3.Br. 5th W.Y.R. Regiment (Captain ?) acting as 115th (Brig) 2/6th White Fork. Our Fighting Patrol during the night - Disposition: Right, C. Left, B. Right Support A. Left Support D. B.H.Q. on LA BELLE ALLIANCE. Battalion in the line. F.B.C.M. Lt T. Davies on ?? Right Support Battalion H.Q.	
	9th		At stand ??. 6.0 a.m. from leave. Battalion in the line. Orders received of two Phase line Co. by the two Support Co's. Positions and relief effected. 2/6th J.K. Morris and T.R. ??Williams on Patrol. Battalion in the Line. One relief Coy received - Officer of Patrol. ?? Norse ???? reconnoitred the Line. 2/6th H.M. ??	
	10th			
	11th		??in Patrol. Corporal ?? one O.R. wounded. 2/6th I.P. ???? attached to Support Battalion as Liaison Officer.	

WAR DIARY
INTELLIGENCE SUMMARY
(Erase heading not required.)

Army Form C. 2118.

Place	Date	Hour	Summary of Events and Information	Remarks and references to Appendices
YPRES (area)	Aug 1917 12th		Actg/ Maj. Jendrich – Capt. T.A. Higbee proceeded to take over Camp G. Lewis Gunners return by lorry. Battalion relief by 13th Royal Sussex commenced at 5 p.m. – complete at 7 p.m. Battalion marched to CAMP G. arriving at 11 p.m. Battalion in Camp G. relieving 1/18 Yorks in Divisional Reserve.	
	13th		Superintending of dusting morning – Capt T.A. Higbee proceeded to take over ROUSSEL FARM CAMP. Battalion paraded at 4 p.m. in G. CAMP and marched to ROUSSEL FARM (Sheet 28 N.W. B.13.a.3.6) Battalion complete in camp at about 6.30 p.m.	
	14th		Day spent in clearing camp, conducting latrines, new sitting for men and general improvement. Battalion billets CLEVERDINGHE(?)	
	15th		Physical Training, Musketry and Bombing – Lewis Gunners and Specials under their respective Officers. Arrangements with 71 D.L.I. /owner on Battalion single Jacques 140 D.R.	

Place	Date	Hour	Summary of Events and Information	Remarks and references to Appendices
YPRES	Aug 16		Training as in previous day. New draft under R.S.M. Wynn joined 330 O.R.	
	17		Sunday - Church Parade - C. of E., R.C. and Nonconformists in the camp. Inspection of Box Respirators - Box Respirators drill - Lecture Inspection of maps. Rifles were received for Jordan - Battalion paraded at 4 p.m. and marched to SHORT FARM area (3.10c.2.4.) being the Support area of BOISINGHE Sector (ready there on five the Essex/Bombs to give [illegible]	
	18		Cleaning trenches, dugouts etc. Musketry, arm drill etc. Major Edwards rejoined from leave. Reign assigned D.O.C.	
	19		Physical drill, bayonet fighting, musketry, bomb throwing etc. Capt Graham and 2/Lt [illegible] proceeded on leave.	
	20		Training as before	
	21		Physical drill, Inspection of Box Respirators, Box Respirator drill, Bomb throwing, rapid wiring. Coy commanders lecture	

Place	Date	Hour	Summary of Events and Information	Remarks and references to Appendices
YPRES	Dec 2/15 (cont)		Officers from Signalling Office with runners passed round first line to arrange details of relief - Operation orders issued.	
	3rd		Operation orders published - Reconnain parties to front line BOESINGHE Bulb. relieving 10th Battalion P.N.B. Regt composed 7.30 p.m. Dispositions: Rifle Coy, A: Echelon Coy, B: Left Coy, D. C Coy in support in X14 and X5. Battalion HQ in BOESINGH 2 CHATEAU (B 11 & B 8.4) on the left of the Battalion was the 3rd Battalion of the 2nd Regt of Chasseurs à Pied of the Belgian Army - On the right was the 16th Canadian Rifle Brigade. At 9 a.m. enemy opened an intermittent shelling and of medium heavy nature upon our front and support lines and communication trenches forward of Coy HQrs. and a desultory bombardment with H.E. and Shrapnel of the VILLAGE LINES. He also made great use of rifle grenades and machine guns, which latter swept our front line parapets. This bombardment continued until 3.0 a.m. on December 4th. The enemy (who is believed to have moved a new lot of troops for purpose of assaulting ours)	

Army Form C. 2118.

WAR DIARY or INTELLIGENCE SUMMARY

Place	Date	Hour	Summary of Events and Information	Remarks and references to Appendices
YPRES	Nov 27th (contd)		...enter our front line about B12 to H4. It was subsequently discovered that 2 N.C.O.'s and 10 men were missing - two officers - Capt. A. Morgan Williams and 2nd Lt. J. Davies - and 2 men wounded (Capt. A. Morgan Williams). Some of the missing men are subsequently found killed and wounded by the bombardment. This sector had just been taken over from the trench mortars the preliminaries of the line had not been appreciated by anybody. The Canal was recognised as an obstacle. These events, which occurred the night we took over the line from the 10th S.W.B. proved the Canal to be a great obstacle and proved its lia to be a particularly easy one to raid. Given an intense bombardment of French Mortars, the enemy could charge the bank in the railway bridge or cross on rafts without being seen whilst on the same time his machine guns could sweep our parapets from our to left down effectively keeping sentries heads down. Given the hope of the bank this machine gun fire could be kept up until the enemy party were within few yards of our bombing post. What seems to be the weakness of our posts	

WAR DIARY or INTELLIGENCE SUMMARY

Army Form C. 2118.

Place	Date	Hour	Summary of Events and Information	Remarks and references to Appendices
YPRES.	Dec. 2nd (contd)		is enfilement by the foot where the enemy must have crossed opposite the bombing post on the bridge and jumpers straight on to them swum something already evacuated. The Lewis Gun post 50 yards to the right, with its 5 occupants have been completely wiped out by a trench mortar. The Lewis Gun post 50 yards to the left has been split up several times by its commander, this man going to the left, the Corporal, three men and the gun going to the right. They must have rushed, carrying the gun, straight into the raiding party. This shows that at the time the raiding party entered our line there were no sentries out at the entrance of the bombing post. For a distance of 100 yards on either side of the point of entry there was a sad night and the trench and its bombardment intense so it is not surprising that the enemy were not sighted or even seen. A wounded man in the bombing post 110 yards right of the bridge said that he saw the Germans retiring on masse and firing on them – Captain Kirkman witnessing the wiping out of the Garrison from his observation post the Germans were not	

2449 Wt. W14957/M90 759,000 1/16 J.B.C. & A. Forms/C.2118/12.

WAR DIARY or INTELLIGENCE SUMMARY

Army Form C. 2118.

Place	Date	Hour	Summary of Events and Information	Remarks and references to Appendices
YPRES	Sep 23rd 1916 (contd)		Men in and out then he had been hit by a Rifle Grenade. This was later proved false, as a number trickled into return from his body in hospital. The behaviour of the men was excellent exceeding every expectation. The line had been held by the 39th Division for a month and at Leeuw (left the sub sector) known in the difficulties of finding the compliment this line had not been appreciated in the least. Since the event its line has been reconnoitred by our the Staff from army commands and the system of defence is being entirely re-organized. From 2 p.m. to 3 p.m. the artillery of the Group bombarded the enemy support and communication trenches. The minimum arm lype trench mortars similarly bombarded the enemy's front line and communication trenches. The enemy's retaliation was weak and was no damage. During this bombardment the whole of our front line was cleared	

Army Form C. 2118.

WAR DIARY or INTELLIGENCE SUMMARY

(Erase heading not required.)

Instructions regarding War Diaries and Intelligence Summaries are contained in F. S., Regs., Part II. and the Staff Manual respectively. Title Pages will be prepared in manuscript.

Place	Date	Hour	Summary of Events and Information	Remarks and references to Appendices
YPRES	Dec 24th		Comparatively quiet day - little artillery activity on part of enemy. Brisk rifle firing in opening envelope sent to Huns who sang communication trench by enemy last night.	
	Dec 25th		Christmas day. In the early hours the enemy shouted a wish to be friendly, went out to an man "Merry Xmas Tommy, Merry Xmas Tommy". A happy Christmas to you. I hope we will look to friends. The exact English days, including "Turn down the King" "accompanied by a full band orchestra. Two of New Places themselves, and were, and welcomed before a shot could be fired or seen - during the morning and again as night the chaplain, Capt. R. Whitworth, held holy communion services in the fire line - Brit has largely attended. Divine service was held in Company Headquarters. Are very an artillery maintained a slow bombardment of the enemy's trenches assisted by machine and light trench mortars and rifle grenades. The enemy did not retaliate until 4.15 p.m. when he sent a number of Minenwerfer	

2449 Wt. W14957/M90 750,000 1/16 J.B.C. & A. Forms/C.2118/12.

WAR DIARY
INTELLIGENCE SUMMARY
(Erase heading not required.)

Army Form C. 2118.

Place	Date	Hour	Summary of Events and Information	Remarks and references to Appendices
YPRES	Dec 25th (contd)		and Englishmen heard carols in the neighbourhood of our front line. Our artillery replied vigorously - during the evening the enemy fired a salvo of Shrapnel over the village time again. An enemy aeroplane flew over and also using of guns heard. Battalion men to relief received and published. The Battalion was relieved by the 10th Battalion S.W.B's. Relief complete at 7.30 p.m. Battalion proceeded to the support billets at BLUET FARM.	
	27th		Inspection arms Company armourers and cleaning up. Large fatigue parties found in fire trenches and communication trenches.	
	28th		Church and musketry parade. 6 officers of 14th Hants Regt inspected the various posts of the battalion from the Canal area. Communion service by Capt. Cox Havard C.F. Bn C.of E.F. Church men for self recruit.	
	29th		Training as above. Capt. T. A. Hyde and 1 N.C.O. per Company proceeded to BOLLEZEELE to attend lurking party.	

Army Form C. 2118.

WAR DIARY
or
INTELLIGENCE SUMMARY

(Erase heading not required.)

Place	Date	Hour	Summary of Events and Information	Remarks and references to Appendices
YPRES.	Aug 30th		Transport transport started for BOLLEZEELE at 7. a.m. The Battalion (by Companies) left BLUET FARM between 6/m and 7/f m and marched to POPERINGHE when they entrained in two trains for BOLLEZEELE at 11 p.m. and 11.10 p.m. arriving there at 2.45 a.m. and 3 a.m. (31st) The Companies then marched to their first and transport arrived at BOLLEZEELE at 5.30 p.m	
	Aug 31st		Sunday. Cleaning up and the inspection under Company arrangements.	

H.S.Taylor Lt Col.
Cmdg 17 R.W.F.

17 Bn. R. Welsh Fus.
Vol 14

14 G
5 sheets

WAR DIARY or INTELLIGENCE SUMMARY
(Erase heading not required.)

Army Form C. 2118.

Place	Date	Hour	Summary of Events and Information	Remarks and references to Appendices
BOLLEZEELE	1917 Jan 1		Battalion in Corps Reserve. Day devoted to training. Physical Training, 8 a.m. Kit drill, Company drill, Arm drill, musketry, entrenching & wiring parties, Lewis Gun message, kit inspection.	
	Jan 2		Battalion to Baths. Training as on previous day. Half the Officers absent out a tactical exercise in the afternoon. 2/Lt R. Tandagra returned from hospital.	
	Jan 3		Training continued morning bomb throwing and competitions. Afternoon devoted to Sport. Bomb C.O.'s inspection further models — A and D Co's. Half Officers tactical exercise. B.Coy firing on range musketry competitions. 2/Lt T.E. Ashcroft transferred to D Coy.	
	Jan 14		Training: Physical training, Gas defence drill, rapid entrenching with attacking post. Bomb throwing, rapid wiring. Afternoon devoted to Sport. Inspecting Capt Waddin and 20 O.R. proceeded on leave. C. Coy fired on range in afternoon. Capt Daniel, A and D Coy's attack from trenches with enemy trenches re-organising of position. I and C Co's rapid wiring.	
	Jan 5		Training: A and D Co's attack from trenches with enemy trenches. Afternoon, the and reorganisation of position. I and C Co's rapid wiring. Army Commander inspected the Battalion at work on the training area. A and D Co's entrenching drill. B and C Co's rapid wiring. R.S.M. de Chaum N.C.O.'s on the Lewis Gun.	

WAR DIARY
INTELLIGENCE SUMMARY
(Erase heading not required.)

Army Form C. 2118.

Place	Date	Hour	Summary of Events and Information	Remarks and references to Appendices
BOLLEZEELE	1919 Jan 6.		Training; Musketry, Rapid Loading, fire control. Company attacks on enemy knolls. Afternoon; Inter-Company football matches.	
	Jan 7.		(Sunday) Church Services. In the recommendations, Inspection of Battalion marching past from Church - Lecture Inspection of Companies. Inter-Company football matches; Tug-of-war Competitions, Cross-country running, Boxing.	
	Jan 8.		Battalion and Company outpost scheme. Afternoon; Sports - Lectures by Company Commanders on "Advanced Guards".	
	Jan 9.		Kit inspection. Battalion route march via Knupset; advance guard on road and in open country - Route WINDMILL, VOLKERINCKHOVE, TRAINING AREA, MERCKEGHEM. Afternoon; Cross-country running and Bayonet fighting - Lecture to officers by C.O. on "Battalion in advance".	
	Jan 10.		Training; Section Bomb instruction; bombs (practice with dummy bombs and Bayonet Scheme (Bayonet in attack) on Enemy outpost training. Afternoon; Company sports to enforce parade competitions - are to be postponed owing to unfavourable state of the ground - Route BOLLEZEELE, LE Asselin route march - Inspection on the march.	
	Jan 11.		NIELSBRUGGE, POUBROUCK, G.9 & 8.8. VOLCKERINCKHOVE - Route taken L. Lewis gunners fire drill, not route practice. Afternoon; Tug of war competitions.	

WAR DIARY or INTELLIGENCE SUMMARY

Army Form C. 2118.

Place	Date	Hour	Summary of Events and Information	Remarks and references to Appendices
BOLLEZEELE	Jan 12		Bombing, Lewis Gun instruction, bayonet fighting and musketry. Afternoon: Brigade Scheme again postponed owing to inclement weather.	
	Jan 13		Programme: Bullpom Scheme with Battalion in the outpost line — Cancelled by G.O.C. owing to rain — Bathing and kit/box repairs.	
	Jan 14		Operation orders received. Battalion entrained at BOLLEZEELE for POPERINGHE relieving a Battalion of the 117th Brigade — 10th New K.L.R. took over BOHEZELE Billets — Battalion marched from POPERINGHE to CAMP G.	
YPRES (POPERINGHE CAMP G.)	Jan 15		Morning: bombing, musketry, bayonet fighting and company drill. Afternoon: Cleaning up billets and huts at 2.45 to march to L. Line.	
YPRES (BOESINGHE L. LINE)	Jan 16		Battalion in L. LINE. Distribution: 2 Companies (less one platoon) at ELVERDINGHE (L.6) – Four Platoons at BURGOMASTER FM and MACHINE GUN FARM (L.2) (L.3). Two platoons at MEMAHON FARM (L.2). Two platoons at SEMINAIRE (L.4). Two platoons at TRIEGERSBURG CHATEAU (L.10) not nearer us in the platoon. Headquarters with particulars hereon as to relieving Battalion — Capt R.L. Williams in charge of ELVERDINGHE DEFENCES.	
	Jan 17		Battalion working on L. defences 9 a.m. to 12.30 p.m., 1.30 p.m. to 4.30 p.m.	
	Jan 18		Work as on previous day.	

Army Form C. 2118.

WAR DIARY
or
INTELLIGENCE SUMMARY
(Erase heading not required.)

Instructions regarding War Diaries and Intelligence Summaries are contained in F. S. Regs., Part II. and the Staff Manual respectively. Title Pages will be prepared in manuscript.

Place	Date	Hour	Summary of Events and Information	Remarks and references to Appendices
YPRES (TRENCHES AND LINE)	Jan 20		Work on L. DEFENCES as in previous days. The following officer and O.R. mentioned in Inspection Capt R.L. WILLIAMS. 25840 SGT. J.L. OWEN, B Coy. 26088 Pte E.H. KEMP, B Coy.	
	Jan 21		(Sunday) Work on L. DEFENCES suspended. Church Parade.	
	Jan 22		Work on L. DEFENCES resumed as on 20th. F.G.C.M. present over by Major Angus 17th Welch Regt convened for trial of Pte W. Hutton B Coy. charged with 'having injured without leave.'	
	Jan 23		Work on L. DEFENCES. Reinforcements of officers and O.R. arrived.	
	Jan 24		Work on L. DEFENCES. Hostile aeroplanes very active. Three of our machines brought down on our Machine Gun Fire. Transport thieves.	
	Jan 25		Work on L. DEFENCES. 8 p.m. Shrapnel thrown somewhat in rt. of (?) pres (neighbourhood) Battalion Stood to 15 - 10 p.m. Silent alarm whereon new gas front been shewn.	
	Jan 26		Work on L. DEFENCES - 10.15 p.m. Gas alarm given and defences manned - Companies reporting all posts manned by 10.45 p.m.	
	27th		Work on L. DEFENCES - Operation orders received. Battalion to be relieved by 10th S.W.B's and to relieve 11th S.W.B's in rot support line.	

WAR DIARY or INTELLIGENCE SUMMARY

Army Form C. 2118.

Place	Date	Hour	Summary of Events and Information	Remarks and references to Appendices
YPRES (BOESINGHE L.LINE.)	Jan 28		(Sunday) Work suspended on L. DEFENCES - Church Parades - Battalion nothing at FLYERDINGHE - Battalion relieved in L.LINE by 10th S.W.B. and moved into support in BOESINGHE SECTOR, relieving 11th S.W.B. Dispositions: Battalion H.Q. and C. and D. Coys at BLEUET FARM. A. and B. Companies in X.LINE. Relief complete 8.30 p.m.	
BOESINGHE (SUPPORT LINE).	Jan 29th		Working parties provided 9.30 p.m.(28th) to 2.30 a.m.(29th). Inspection of arms, equipment and box respirators. 2/Lt L.E.H. WILLIAMS reported for duty and was posted to D. Coy. 2/Lt P.G. HARRIS transferred from D. Coy to A. Coy. Working parties as per working-party table provided 5.30 p.m. to 9.30 p.m.	
	Jan 30th	1.30 a.m.	Intense trench mortar bombardment of Belgians at HET SAS - Heavy Belgian retaliation, in which some of our guns joined. Musketry, Bayonet fighting, Physical Training at 9.30 a.m. to 12.30 p.m. F.G.C.M.(Maxieres on by Major Angus, 17th Welch Regt.) for trial of Lce Bnty charged with being absent without leave. Working parties 5.30 p.m. to 9.30 p.m.	
	Jan 31st		Training 9.30 a.m. to 12.30 p.m. Working parties 5.30 p.m. to 9.30 p.m. Operation orders received. Battalion to relieve 11th S.W.B. in front line on night of 1st/2nd July 1917. Orders subsequently received postponing relief to night of 2nd/3rd July 1917.	

W. J. Taylor Lt Col
Comdg 17 R.W. Ldd Fusiliers

Army Form C. 2118.

WAR DIARY or INTELLIGENCE SUMMARY

(Erase heading not required.)

17 Bn. R.W.F.

Vol. 16

Place	Date	Hour	Summary of Events and Information	Remarks and references to Appendices
YPRES (BOESINGHE) BLEUET FARM B10C 7.4.)	1917 July 1.		Battalion at BLEUET FARM. Paraded under Company arrangements. Quiet day at BLEUET FARM. Parties under Company arrangements. Battalion moved to front line BOESINGHE SECTOR, relieving 11th S.W.B's. Relief completed reported to Brigade at 9.30 p.m. Very heavy frost – Canal frozen – Little enemy activity. L.H.V.5 on S. LINE and occasional hostile m/g fire. Aeroplane heard overhead at 1 a.m. Heavy bombardment Belgians to our left 4 a.m. to 5.30 a.m. Also shot shell of artillery shafts on Belgians to our right at 5.30 a.m. in preparation of Belgians Battalion. Activity on right Brigade front to our right. B.Coy BOESINGHE REDOUBT. Line on our left 3rd Gds. Brigade A batt. BOESINGHE C.Coy VILLAGE LINE. D.Coy VILLAGE STREET and RAILWAY STREET. Enemy occasional shot bursts of enemy L.M.V.5 on VILLAGE STREET and RAILWAY STREET. Enemy aeroplane overhead several times during day – Some artillery activity on our part, especially heavy artillery whose fire appeared to be directed on enemy front about CAESAR'S NOSE (C.13.d.8.8) Enemy working parties as apparent by L.G. fire during the night. Enemy called several times to us.	
	July 3.		Very little enemy activity. Enemy sniping heavily – Our sentries shown are hit. Enemy machine guns active during night. Enemy one apparent great opposite our off Coy. front that went as good opposite left Company's many gaps. Enemy parties attempting to rush at rifle our own front as by our Lewis Gun fire.	
	July 4.			
	July 5.		Enemy working party (1.15 a.m.) fired upon by our Lewis Guns; both gun in place below – Fired upon both riffle fire nemes. Enemy retaliated with L.T.M's. at 1 p.m. enemy fired about twelve 5.5's at about B.12.C.Central. Several "duds". Our heavy artillery active.	

WAR DIARY or INTELLIGENCE SUMMARY

Army Form C. 2118.

19. R.W.F.
February 1917.

Place	Date	Hour	Summary of Events and Information	Remarks and references to Appendices
BOESINGHE	Feb 6.	12.45 p.m.	Enemy sent over several rifle grenades. Lt replied with 2 rifle grenades. No 3 and Hales. No. 20 and silenced him. Battalion relieved and moved back to ROUSSEL FARM (in reserve).	
	Feb 7.		Working parties on Railway Construction from 8 a.m. Remainder of Battalion cleaning up and previous route Company arrangements.	
	Feb 8.		Working parties on Railway Construction — Enemy shelled Railway near ROUSSEL FARM — also camp occupied by 115 M.G. Company with about 250 5.9's.	
	Feb 9.		Working parties on Railway Construction and Riviere under Company arrangements.	
	Feb 10.		Working parties on Railway Construction and Riviere under Company arrangements. Battalion relieved 11th S.W.B.'s at BLEUET FARM. (B10.C.7.4) in Support. Lent 4 groups of communication (one New Wipers) between Battalions and Brigade. Relieved 7 p.m. and 8 p.m. 28 message sent by runners from and Lamps to Brigade and Companies. C Coy, X HnE (right): D Coy, X HnE (left): A and Boys BLEUET FARM ahead. Disposition of Companies.	
	Feb 11.		Working parties as for Feb 10, and parties under Company arrangements.	
	Feb 12		Ditto —	

WAR DIARY or INTELLIGENCE SUMMARY

Army Form C. 2118.

17 R.W.F.
January 1917.

Place	Date	Hour	Summary of Events and Information	Remarks and references to Appendices
BOESINGHE (BRUIT FM)	July 13		Working parties. Snipers under Company arrangements. Enemy shelled DUMP at the GASOMETER during the night.	
	July 14		Battalion relieved 11th S.W.B's in front line, BOESINGHE sectn. Enemy active. Heavy T.M's at intervals during the night. Casualties 2 killed, 3 wounded. Our Battn H.Q. at B9g 55.85 to right B9g V2.95 on right; C. Coy BOESINGHE REDOUBT. No damage VILLAGE STREET from CONTRIVANCE CHATEAU not intermittently all day. L.M.V.	
	July 15		Our artillery retaliated. Enemy "pineapples" became fell near a Company H.Q. in VILLAGE STREET, wounding three men. Considerable enemy aerial activity over our lines - but 8 our machines kept down under escort behind our lines. Enemy machine kept over our lines behind own lines - patrol work. Continuous shell bombardment all day by our artillery of KRUPP SALIENT (B14a). At night enemy wiring parties dispersed by L.G. fire.	
	July 16		Between 7 a.m. and 1 p.m. enemy fired about 75 L.M.V's on b. VILLAGE STREET. Also a few M.2. Our artillery retaliated. Communication severed at times. Enemy shewed desire to photograph; crossing over our lines to our rear. Enemy machine gun fire on our wiring parties.	
	July 17		From 8 a.m. to 12.30 p.m. enemy shelled VILLAGE STREET intermittently with L.M.V. (H.E. and Shrapnel) - 1 officer wounded, 1 man killed. Our artillery retaliated	

WAR DIARY or INTELLIGENCE SUMMARY

Army Form C. 2118.

17 Rn. J.
February (?)

Place	Date	Hour	Summary of Events and Information	Remarks and references to Appendices
BOESINGHE	July 17.		and 50 4.5's which silenced the enemy. Enemy shelled ELVERDINGHE-BOESINGHE road during noon and during evening.	
	July 18.		Enemy front immediately known heavily bombarded at 3.19 a.m. Enemy front in communication with a near by us on the next bye-one front. Enemy shelled VILLAGE STREET (near CHURCH) intermittently during morning. Battalion on our bonstjun advance line. Quiet spent. Battalion relieved by 10th Battalion S.W.B's and marched into X.CAMP. (A14C). In reserve.	
	July 19.		Working parties in Ancillary Amplrichin and Pioneer work company arrangements. Baths and bathing at POPERINGHE.	
	July 20.		ditto	
	July 21.		ditto	
	July 22.		Battalion relieved 11th S.W.B's at BLEUET FARM. Disposition of Companies: A Coy x HN F (n g w). PAH ADOU FM. B Coy. H 2 pillboxes B9C10.H. D Coy. B 10.6.27. C Coy. & Shelines. Working parties and katring under company arrangements.	
	July 23.		ditto.	
	July 24.		ditto.	
	July 25th		Sunday. Church Parade and denominations. Working parties in X.LINE.	
	July 26th		Battalion relieved in support by 10th S.W.B's and moved into front line, relieving 11th S.W.B's. New Company HdQtrs 8.38 a.m. Enemy shelled ELVERDINGHE-BOESINGHE road during the evening. Company disposition. D. Coy. Right front half. C Coy left front half. A Coy Village but B Coy Chateau kymants. Relief on our left 2nd Regt de Carabiners found on our right 16th Rn. J.	

2449 Wt. W14957/Mgo 750,000 1/16 J.B.C. & A. Forms/C.2118/12.

Army Form C. 2118.

WAR DIARY
or
INTELLIGENCE SUMMARY
(Erase heading not required.)

17 Bn d
February 1917

Place	Date	Hour	Summary of Events and Information	Remarks and references to Appendices
BOESINGHE	Feb 2nd		During the morning the enemy fired about 30 rounds of L.H.V. in the vicinity of the CHURCH - On retaliation being asked for, our 18 pr and howitzers opened fire very promptly and effectively. Silencing the enemy. In the early hours of the morning two officers patrols rep'd in our lines -	
	4.15 PM	9.15 pm	Enemy opened fire on CHATEAU GROUNDS with Heavy T.M's and on VILLAGE STREET with Rifle grenades. Artillery retaliation was called for and obtained. Our Medium and Light T.M's also replied - Enemy T.M activity continued, principally in BRIDGE ST (near CHATEAU) RAILWAY ST. HUNTER ST - vicinity of CHURCH and FRONT LINE (B12.1) Our return T.M emplacements came in for considerable attention - Enemy fire slackened about 11 p.m except intermittent bursts military activity until 4.45 a.m. Cannonade. Enemy had one No1 Post and front near left - Bn O.R killed - 4 O.R wounded - Damage - RAILWAY STREET damaged in two places - BRIDGE ST (near of B10.1 knocked in - CHATEAU) in four places and HUNTER STREET in one place. Damaged trenches have cleared by working parties during the night	

H.J. Taylor Lt Col
Commdg 17 Rn J
1.3.19??

WAR DIARY
INTELLIGENCE SUMMARY

Army Form C. 2118.

17th Bn Royal Welsh Fusiliers

Vol 16

Place	Date	Hour	Summary of Events and Information	Remarks and references to Appendices
YPRES Boesinghe (Belgium) 28 N.W.B.II.b	1st March		St David's Day - Battalion in front line. Coy dispositions: D Coy Right front. C Coy Left front. A Coy Village Lines. B Coy Chateau Grounds. Lieut on our left 4th Dorsetshire. (Lieut gr Carabiniers) Lieut on our right 16th R.N.F. Two. Enemy heavy artillery action all day in duration of ELVERDINGHE. Considerable aerial activity.	
	2nd March		Quiet day - between Patrol across to our "Caux over Comrade". Battalion relieved by 10th Battn 3rd Br. R.W.F. Complete 9th 6th Inn. Battalion out at reserve at X Camp (A16.c.3.3.) M.O. was sent during relief.	
X Camp (A16 C.2.3.)	3rd March		Working parties for Railway (Australia) supplied by A B & C Coys. D Coy carried on with Baths and Recreational Competitions. Camp Band at our Range. 2/Lieut Potrock rejoined for duty from England and posted to B Coy. Court of Enquiry held at Divisional During Sir into circumstances attending wounding at 55640 Pte Ambrose E of Knobhill while examining his own rifle. Capt Rogerson rejoined from command Sanitation at Gaysbrouck.	
	4th March		Sunday - Church parade all denominations. No Roman Catholic work. Inspection of huts by Reynolds and P B. & Co. Inspection of Battalion by H.O. Celebration of St David's Day. Men were provided with special fare at meals, and a Concert was held. Officers Dinner: Regimental Guests. Enemy bombs returned.	16P 10 sheets

WAR DIARY
INTELLIGENCE SUMMARY 17th Royal Welsh Fusiliers

Army Form C. 2118.

Place	Date 1917	Hour	Summary of Events and Information	Remarks and references to Appendices
X Camp A.6.c.3.3.	5th March		Working parties from A, B & D Coys for Railway Construction. C Coy carried on Reservational Competition in Camp. Capt. R.P. Daniel left for Reg. Stretcher Bearers Course. 2/Lieut. J.B. Hartley left Stores for course of Instruction in Transport Duties.	
	6th March		C Coy proceeded to huts at Roussel Farm (B.18.6.5.8.) Working parties for Railway Construction work found by B C & D Coys. A Coy carried on Recreational Competition in Camp. A Coy and H.Q. bathed at ELVERDINGHE during afternoon. Battalion moved up into Support, relieving 16th Batt. Welch Regt at BLUET FARM and X Line. Dispositions of Companies:— A Coy BARN FARM, B Coy at PARADOU FARM, D Coy in X Line (Right) C Coy in X Line (Left). Battalion H.Q. at BLUET FARM. Relief complete at 7pm.	
BLUET FARM B.10.c.3.3.	7th March		Working parties as per Bar Work Table. Nineng X Line and defensive flanks.	
	8th March		Working parties as per Bar Work Table. Nineng X Line and defensive flanks. Baths at Elverdinghe utilized by B C & D Coys in relays. Working parties as per Bar Work Table. Situation normal. Batts at Elverdinghe Corner hill	

Lias et les Officers
L.W.M.

WAR DIARY
INTELLIGENCE SUMMARY

17th Royal Welsh Fusiliers

Army Form C. 2118.

Place	Date	Hour	Summary of Events and Information	Remarks and references to Appendices
BOESINGHE Bs d 2 8. March	10th		Working parties as per Boe Work Table. 08 Italians relieved us 10th Batt S.H. Regt. and relieved 16th Batt Welsh Regt in Front Line. Disposition of Companies: B Coy Right front; A Coy, Left front; C Coy VILLAGE 'ST'. D Coy BOESINGHE REDOUBT. Batt. H.Q. BOESINGHE CHATEAU. Relief complete 8.30 p.m. that on our left 4th Carabiniers (Belgian Army) - that on our right 16th Batt R.W. Fus. One O.R. wounded during relief - cont of enquiry convened and held to enquire into circumstances of the wounding. 2s0.03 Pte H. Clewett. Usual working parties during night. Moonlight rendering front line moving extremely difficult, every confined to during round Sentry Posts and in S" line. Usual working parties. Gt Aerial activity, so many as eight enemy machines being observed in the air simultaneously - Many air-fights. Two machines brought down completely out of control in the direction of YPRES (Nationality not ascertainable). Our heavy artillery	J.W.B.
	11th			

WAR DIARY
INTELLIGENCE SUMMARY 17th Royal Welsh Fusiliers

Army Form C. 2118.

Place	Date 1917	Hour	Summary of Events and Information	Remarks and references to Appendices
(Continued)	March 11		Bombarded enemy support line intermittently all day. At night enemy round Sentry Posts and before 'S' line.	
	12		Issued working parties. Very little enemy activity on our front except rifle grenades — retaliation for our grenades, to which we replied with trench mortar grenades — no response being made by the enemy. Our 18 pdrs shelled vicinity of STEAM MILL during the afternoon. 2/Lieut Seed rejoined for duty on leaving Hospital. At night enemy carried on in S line and in front of and round posts. Usual Working parties. Some enemy aerial activity — his machines flying lower than usual. Our A.A. Guns prevented enemy machines crossing our lines. One O.R. killed by enemy sniper. Usual working parties at night. 2 Carabinieri with 4th Carabinieri with a view to preventing 2 Carabinieri now left, relieved by 4th Carabinieri with a view to preventing espionage, arrangements made though Brigade whereby only authorised persons with the password) where to be allowed in our Area.	
	13		Quiet day. Battalion Relieved by 10th Batt. Sh. B. and 3 Coys proceed to X Camp, D Coy proceeding to Rouen Farm. Relief complete 8 p.m. 2/Lieut Phillips Inst.	

X Camp
A N.C. 3.3

WAR DIARY

INTELLIGENCE SUMMARY 17th Battn. Royal Welsh Fusiliers

Army Form C. 2118.

Place	Date	Hour	Summary of Events and Information	Remarks and references to Appendices
X Camp A.16.c.3.3.	14th		S.T. reported for duty.	
	15th		Working parties of 4 Officers & 250 O.R. for burying Corpses. Supterns. Remainder of men in Camp Training in Musketry, Bombing, Rifle Grenades, Bayonet Fighting; one hour on each subject. Lectures to Officers by C.O. on "Training Beyond Conference in Outpost duty".	
	16		Working parties and training as above, different men being left in Camp for training. Football Match A Coy v C Coy in afternoon. 2/Lt W S Jones attached 118 T.M.B. for duty with Divnl Sniping Coy. 2/Lt R Stock attached for duty with 118 T.M.B. Lecture to Officers by C.O. on "Zone Control". Major St Edmunds proceeded home.	
	17th		Working parties and training as before. Tactical exercise for Officers under C.O.: Football Match C Coy v Burne Brunonian Column. Rained & snow — 2 good each. —	
ELVERDINGHE DEFENCES (B.14 & Outpost) TO L.4. (H.12 a. 4.8.)	18		(Sunday) Working parties as before. Battalion proceeded to Line - Preparation of Companies A & B Coy ELVERDINGHE DEFENCES. C Coy 2 platoons at L2 (H.11 a.6.8.) and 2 platoons at L8 (C.5.2.3.) D Coy 3 platoons at L4 (H.12.a.4.8.) and 1 at I.A St.	

WAR DIARY or INTELLIGENCE SUMMARY

17th Royal Welsh Fusiliers

Army Form C. 2118.

Place	Date	Hour	Summary of Events and Information	Remarks and references to Appendices
ELVERDINGHE But extend L4 to H12 c 4.5	18		One platoon at L10 (H66 4.5) Battalion HQ at L8 (Machine Gun Farm) Battalion reported in	
		Until 10 p.m.	Working parties on defences. Relays of men for Battn at ELVERDINGHE. Men who could be spared from working parties trained in Rifle Grenades + Lewis Gun. Enemy shelled L2 lightly, also vicinity of L8. No damage & no casualties. Operation Orders received for Battalion to relieve 16th Battn R.W.F. in Front Line (SKIPTON ROAD and CANAL)	
	20		Working parties on defences. CO, Company Officers etc reconnoitred new sector to be taken over. Operation Orders received. Battalion to relieve 6th R.W.F. in front line (new Canal Section from C13 2 inclusive to C 7 5 inclusive) and 10th S.W.B's in support. Section to be under the command of Lt Col J. Hayes DSO 14th Batt Welsh Regt with temporary staff. Section HQ at du Infantry Bar HQ at C19 c 4 3. Divisional sector divided on new system. Right sector (1 Brigade) C21 3 to C13 1 inclusive. Centre section (2 Battalions) C13 2 to C 7 5 inclusive. Left sector (2 Battalions) B12 1 to B 6 4 inclusive. Four Battalions at BOLLEZEELE. Bn A/Sheriff-Roberts rejoined fro	

duty and took command of "D" Coy

WAR DIARY
INTELLIGENCE SUMMARY

1st Battn Royal Welsh Fusiliers

Place	Date 1917	Hour	Summary of Events and Information	Remarks and references to Appendices
CENTRE SECTION CANAL BANK C13 c.1.2.	March 21st		Battalion moved into front line C.T. Section, relieving 16th Battn R.W.F. Coy dispositions: Right front 'C' Coy, Left front 'D' Coy, Right support A Coy, Left support B Coy. Battn H.Q. at Frascati House (C13 c.1.2.) Battalion on our Right 10th Battn Welsh Regt. Battalion on our Left 11th S.W.B. Regt. Battalion in support 10th S.W.B. — Relief complete 10.30pm.	
	22nd		Enemy shelled ESSEX FARM and RAILWAY COTTAGE — during relief — no casualties. Lieut Madsijorio & Lieut L.E. Howard evacuated to Hospital. At 4.15am, enemy opened intense bombardment (Artillery & T.M.) on Battalion on our right. Our artillery opened fire very quickly on S.O.S. Very lights being sent up — including to Artillery covering our front. Enemy ceased at 4.35am. Enemy quiet on our front. Intermittent artillery activity during the day, mainly heavy guns firing well back on each side. Three enemy observation balloons up during the day. At 5.30pm one of them appeared to be signalling to artillery by means of a lamp. Shelled at 10 Officers and 6 O.R. sent out on right Coy front at 11.15pm returning at 1.40am. No enemy details encountered. A fighting patrol stood by for an emergency. At 3pm enemy fired T.M. bombs on our left Coy front. This Ynd.	
CENTRE SECTION CANAL BANK C13 C.1.2	23rd		Quiet morning.	

WAR DIARY

INTELLIGENCE SUMMARY

17th Bttn. Royal Welsh Fusiliers

Army Form C. 2118.

Place	Date	Hour	Summary of Events and Information	Remarks and references to Appendices
CENTRE SECTION CANAL BANK C.8.C.1.2.	March 1917		Demobile into mutual TM and artillery activity on our front and on BOESINGHE FRONT lasting until 7.30 pm. Damage slight on our front. One OR. wounded. Between 9.10 pm enemy shelled CANAL BANK and neighborhood lightly with L.H.V. and shrapnel. No damage and no casualties. Our artillery fired two bursts in retaliation. Patrol of 1 Officer and 6 OR went out from C 9 e.5.2. at 11 pm returning at 1.30 am.	
	24		No enemy activity on our front except aerial activity. Enemy Airmen very active and flying lower than usual and near our front line but not crossing it. Several formations of from 5 to 8 enemy machines observed during the day. Intn: Company relief during evening. A Coy changing places with C Coy on the night, and B Coy with D Coy on the left. "Summer time" came into operation. Watches being put forward 1 hour at 11 pm. Patrol of 1 Officer and 6 OR went out from C 13.10 at 10.55 pm (old time) returning at 2 am (summer time). No enemy encountered.	
	25		At morning "Stand to", a dog was observed in our wire. It was shot and brought in but there were no marks of identification. Enemy working party observed near ARTILLERY WOOD at 7.30 am. Artillery informed and	
CENTRE SECTION CANAL BANK C.13.C.1.2.				

WAR DIARY
INTELLIGENCE SUMMARY
(Erase heading not required.)

Army Form C. 2118.

17th Royal Welsh Fusiliers

Place	Date 1917	Hour	Summary of Events and Information	Remarks and references to Appendices
CENTRE SECTION CANAL BANK C.13.c.1.2	March 25.		dispersed them. Our Aircraft active all day, also, intermittent Artillery activity. No enemy activity on our front except considerable Aerial activity. Numbers of enemy machines observed have increased quantity of late. They fly in larger formations and are at a lower altitude than previously, but rarely cross our line. Two enemy observation balloons up during greater part of the day. 2/Lieut R.E.Williams rejoined for duty from Bombing Course.	
	26		Some mutual artillery activity. No active activity. No damage or casualties. No enemy activity. No damage or casualties. 2/Lt B.Rees to Grenade Course. Battalion relieved in line by 19 Bn S.W.B. and went into support on west side Canal Bank. Battn HQ in same quarters. Carrying and wiring parties supplied according to work Table. Wiring of X line during the night.	
CENTRE SECTION CANAL BANK C.13.C.1.2	27th		Baths in West Side of Canal allotted for use of the Battalion during certain hours daily whilst in support. Several Working Parties and wiring parties (X line.)	
	28th		Baths. Working Wiring parties.	W.S.H.

Army Form C. 2118.

WAR DIARY
INTELLIGENCE SUMMARY 17th Batt. Royal Welsh Fusiliers
(Erase heading not required.)

Instructions regarding War Diaries and Intelligence Summaries are contained in F.S. Regs., Part II. and the Staff Manual respectively. Title Pages will be prepared in manuscript.

Place	Date	Hour	Summary of Events and Information	Remarks and references to Appendices
CENTRE SECTION CANAL BANK C.13.C.1.2.	March 1917 29		2/Lieut Pologh to Musketry Course. 2/Lts S.P. Roberts and R. Buckburn to 38th Divnl School. Ordinary trench Mortar registment during afternoon. Enemy Trench Mortars retaliation on our front and Boesinghe Front.	
		30th	At 4:40am the Battalion stood to, an order from O.C. Centre Section the S.O.S. Signal having been sent up by the front line Battalion on our right. Orders to stand down received at 5 am. Situation having quietened. Both were working and trench parties. 11:50 Our Artillery bombarded KRUPP SALIENT (4 guns) for 20 minutes. Enemy retaliation with Trench Mortars on the front + right Battalion front.	
		31st	Baths and normal working + Wiring parties. Battalion relieved 10th S.W.B. in front line - Disposition of Coys: Right front C Coy; Left front D Coy; Right Support A Coy (Coy HQ now in BUTT 22) Left Support C Coy; B Coy Battalion Headquarters at Frascati House West of Canal (C.13.C.1.2.) Relief complete 9:15 pm. 2/Lieut S.J. Phillips to Lewis Gun Course. Battalion moved left - 13th R.W.F. Battalion moves our right - 11th S.W.B.	W.T.

W.S. Taylor Lieut Col.
Commanding 17th R.W.Fus.
1/4/17.

WAR DIARY
INTELLIGENCE SUMMARY

Army Form C. 2118.

(Erase heading not required.)

17th Bn Royal Welsh Fusiliers

Vol 17

E.H.
17 OP
5 sheets

Place	Date 1917	Hour	Summary of Events and Information	Remarks and references to Appendices
YPRES. VIII Corps. 40th Divn: Centre Sector (SWAANHOF)	April 1st		Battalion in front line. Enemy heavy artillery active on our back area - lights, guns also displayed some activity, apparently registering. No damage or casualties. 2/Lieut GR Battely returned from Transport Course. 2/Lieut S.I. Phillips to Lewis Gun Course.	
	2nd		Enemy's and our heavy artillery again active. 2/Lieut B Rees rejoined from Grenade Course. Interday relief during evening. A&B Companies relieved C&D Coys, who went into support.	
	3rd		Normal artillery activity. 2/Lieut D.G. Everall to hospital. Lg.l G.R. Hopkins attached to B 119 Battery for three days.	
	4th		Enemy shelled CANAL BANK lightly. No casualties. Capt DS Oliver & Lewis Guns School at Tournehem.	
	5th		Battalion relieved by 10th Sh. B and moved into support. All Companies in WEST CANAL BANK. Battalion H.Q. remained at Fusilier House (C.13.c.1.2.).	
	6th		Battalion in support. Battalion bathing at CANAL BANK BATHS. Working parties according to Table and also training. Two O.R's wounded (G.S.W.'s)	
Canal Sect (SWAANHOF)	7th		Working parties as per Table. Training - skirmishing tests (With platoon for Bayonets)	

Army Form C. 2118.

WAR DIARY
or
INTELLIGENCE SUMMARY 17th Bttn Royal Welsh Fusiliers

(Erase heading not required.)

Place	Date	Hour	Summary of Events and Information	Remarks and references to Appendices
Out: Sect. (ZWAAN HOF)	April 7th		Coy still in Recreational Training. No 8 Platoon successful and nominated for both stages of competition. 10 am Test Gas Alarm carried out and result reported to Brigade. 2/Lieut H.G.R.Morgan to hospital.	
	8th		Easter Sunday. Communion Service at 7.20 am & 7.40 am. 2/Lieut B Jones to 2nd Army School. 2/Lieut L.E.S.Williams to Lewis Gun Course at VIII Corps school. Very little aerial activity.	
	9th		F.G.C.M. at Elverdinghe for trial of 25838 Pte W.Williams 17RWF charged with sleeping on his sentry post. Heavy snow during afternoon. No enemy artillery activity until evening. His heavy artillery then on our back areas. 9.30 am Test Gas Alarm. Major C.H.Edwards and 2/Lieut J.P.Williams returned from leave.	
1st Line ELVERDINGHE (B.V. Central) to (M12 M 4.5)	10th		Battalion relieved in support by 15"RWF and moved into the "L" line Battalion Headquarters at Conboires - A Coy ELVERDINGHE. B Coy (last platoon) ELVERDINGHE. B Coy (1 platoon) REIGERSBOURG CHATEAU. C Coy (Hers 1 platoon) L.2. C Coy (1 platoon) L.8 and a guard at 4 OR at L.3. D Coy HQ + 2 platoons at L.4. 2 platoons at L.8. Battalion HQ at Machine Gun Farm (L.8).	

WAR DIARY
INTELLIGENCE SUMMARY

Army Form C. 2118.

17ᵗʰ Battⁿ Royal Welch Fusiliers

Place	Date	Hour	Summary of Events and Information	Remarks and references to Appendices
L. LINE ELVERDINGHE Bn Central to L4 (H12a 4.5)	April 1917 11ᵗʰ		Working parties on Defences and unloading rubble at Ypres. Men not on fatigue, training in accordance with special programme drawn out and which consists of Gas Drill, Lewis Gun instruction, Bombing, Bayonet Fighting, Arm Drill Musketry (including half practice on the Ranges at L8 and L4) and Rifle Grenade instructed. Baths at Elverdinghe.	
	12ᵗʰ		Working parties as per Brigade Tables, and Training. Baths & Elverdinghe.	
	13ᵗʰ		Working parties and training. Arrangements made with O.C. B/19 Battery for an Officer to visit the Battery every day for instruction. Working parties and Training.	
	14ᵗʰ		Lt. J. Gra. Whaug carried out during morning. Enemy bombarded one of our Battery positions near MACHINE GUN FARM at 11 p.m.	
	15ᵗʰ		Sunday. No working parties on defences. Church Services for all denominations	
	16ᵗʰ		Working parties and Training.	
	17ᵗʰ		Working parties and Training. Cap. R.Lloyd Williams granted 7 days special leave to England. Lt. J. Hastings acts as Adjutant during his absence	
	18ᵗʰ		Working parties and training.	
L. LINE ELVERDINGHE Bn Central to L4 (H12a 4.5)	19ᵗʰ		Working parties and training 1 to 12 noon. Major C.H. Edwards proceeded to Commanding Officers Course at VII Corps School. Battⁿ later moved to BLUET FARM area and X Line relieving	

2449 Wt. W14957/M90 750,000 1/16 J.B.C. & A. Forms/C.2118/12.

WAR DIARY
INTELLIGENCE SUMMARY
1st Batt. Royal Welsh Fusiliers

Army Form C. 2118.

(Erase heading not required.)

Place	Date 1917	Hour	Summary of Events and Information	Remarks and references to Appendices
BLEUET FARM B10 C.3.3.	April 19		11 Shot. Disposition of Companies, A Coy & Bn HQ Nr BARN FARM (with Coy HQ at JEANNE MARIE COT) D Coy PARADOU FARM (Battalion HQ at BLEUET FARM.) B Coy & two night, B Coy x two night.	
	20		Working parties as for Brigade. Working Party Table and on maintenance of tramway. Bathing by A Coy on night of X two nights.	
	21		Work, training and training as per Table. One OR to special leave.	
	22		Work, training as per tramway. Church services of all denominations.	
	23		Work & training as per table. Semi Final of Football Competition C Group Coy beat D Coy 16 R.W.F. 2 goals to nil. Major C.H. Edwards returned from Corps School. Capt Olives to Company Commanders Course at VIII Corps School.	
	24		Working Parties and Tramway. Battalion moved to Trench line relieving 10" Batt 8th 13 Dispositions of Coys : D Coy - Right front. C Coy - Left front. A Coy VILLAGE STREET B Coy BOESINGHE REDOUBT. 10 8th 13 home to Bleut Farm in support lives on own night.	
	25		4th R.W.F. trench on own left. 1st Regt of Grenadiers.	
	26		Lieut. R.Llwyd Williams returned from leave. Officer and 26 OR to Elverdinghe Chateau for parties in building pontoon Bridge across R. Experience near Ypres City on	

WAR DIARY or INTELLIGENCE SUMMARY

17th Battn Royal Welsh Fusiliers

(Erase heading not required.)

Army Form C. 2118.

Instructions regarding War Diaries and Intelligence Summaries are contained in F.S. Regs., Part II. and the Staff Manual respectively. Title Pages will be prepared in manuscript.

Place	Date	Hour	Summary of Events and Information	Remarks and references to Appendices
BOESINGHE Bd d 28	April 1917 26		Lake of BOESINGHE CHATEAU at 8.45 pm. Battalion struck off Baths, working parties for the Jambes. Battalion working parties subsisted as usual. Lund on our left (1st Regt of Grenadiers) relieved by 2nd Regt Grenadiers.	
	27		Practice with pontoons & training. C Coy played the DAC in the final of Divisional Football Competition. Result DAC 1 goal C Coy Nil. Capt J A Hughes sent to 46 CCS for Dental Treatment.	
	28		Working parties as above — Inter Coy Relief. Behenonging over with D and A with C.	
	29		Working parties as above. 2/Lieut Stock to General Convent Divisional School.	
	30		Bathing Party to BnHQ preparatory to proceeding to MILLAIN 2/Lieut Stone and party of men to Divisional School to take part in B.F. Competition. Capt J A Hughes from 46 C.C.S.	

W J Taylor
Lieut Col
Commdg 17 RWF

WAR DIARY
or
INTELLIGENCE SUMMARY
(Erase heading not required.)

Army Form C. 2118.

11th Batt. Royal Welsh Fusiliers

Vol 18

Place	Date 1917	Hour	Summary of Events and Information	Remarks and references to Appendices
YPRES VIII Corps 29th Div	1 May		Battalion relieved in front line by 14th Batt. The Welsh Regiment and marched to POPPERINGHE where they billeted for the night at the HOP FACTORY.	
POPPERINGHE Sheet 28 NW	2 May		Battalion entrained at 7.10 a.m. for ESQUELBECQ, from which place they marched to MILLAM F.28&7. arriving in billets about 4 p.m.	
MILLAM F.28 & 7 & (Sheet 27D)	3 May		Training in accordance with Training Programme.	
	4 "		Training as above including Pontoon Bridging and Inter-Coy. Football. C/good. B coy Nil	
	5 "		Training etc. as above.	
	6 "		Sunday. Training suspended — Church Services of all denominations. Brigade Services for C/& B.	
	7 "		Training in accordance with programme. Corps Commander visits Training Area. Inter-Coy Football Match. C Coy 1 goal. B Coy Nil.	
	8 "		Battalion Route March and Training	
	9 "		Training as per programme. Inter-Battalion football. 17 RWF 3 goals - 11 RWB Nil.	
	10 "		Training as per programme	
	11 "		Battalion Route March and Outpost scheme. Aeroplane contact patrol demonstration. Training Area attended by 2nd in Command of Corps Beyond Fripling	

WAR DIARY or INTELLIGENCE SUMMARY

Army Form C. 2118.

17 Bn. Royal Welsh Fusiliers

Place	Date	Hour	Summary of Events and Information	Remarks and references to Appendices
MILLAM France (Nov 27)	11 May		instruction for NCOs in training area. Capt H Sheriff-Roberts & 2nd Lieut HGR Morgan reported from Sick Leave.	
	12 May		Training as per programme. Sports during afternoon. Football Blobs got Company's mill.	
	13 May		Sunday - Church parade, all denominations. Afternoon, Brigade Sports in Training Area. The 2nd Bn had 1st and 2nd place for Heavy Draught Horses and 3rd place for Field Kitchens. Revd R. Webb inducted - Battalion long of War, held up to 10th Sept 13.	
	14 May		Battalion carried out practice attack on Training Area. Capt A.G. Clarkson for Lewis Gunners Course vacated MILLAM	
	15 May		Brigade attack on Training Area with Aeroplane Contact patrol.	
HERZEELE Dior 3.4.	16 " 17 "		Battalion left MILLAM, marching to HERZEELE where it billited for the night. Morning parades under Coy arrangements. Afternoon - Battalion marched to Y Camp (POPERINGHE-WATOU ROAD) arriving at 6.50 p.m.	
Y Camp PROVEN F7-b-1-2	18 "		Battalion marched to PROVEN and went under Canvas. MAJOR C.H. EDWARDS attached to Bn HQ as Instructor of Platoon Commander's Course.	

Army Form C. 2118.

WAR DIARY
or
INTELLIGENCE SUMMARY
(Erase heading not required.)

17" Royal Welsh Fusiliers

Instructions regarding War Diaries and Intelligence Summaries are contained in F. S. Regs., Part II. and the Staff Manual respectively. Title Pages will be prepared in manuscript.

Place	Date	Hour	Summary of Events and Information	Remarks and references to Appendices
PROVEN. F 7 1-1-2	19 May 1917		The whole of the Battalion on working parties on YSER Canal Supply System under Corps Water Supply Officer.	
	20 "		Work as above – Chief pioneers end of working hours.	
	21 "		Work as above – Employed new parade 11am – 12.30pm & 2pm – 4pm. Classes of instruction for Subaltern Officers.	
	22 "		Work and classes as above. Capt. R.H. Williams to assume lt Course at WISQUES.	
	23 "		2/Lieut A. Stone actg Adjutant. Working parties supplied by A Coy; O/C. Coys training. D Coy bathed at LOVIE Bath and clothes and disinfector.	
CARDOEN FM 24 " (Sheet 28 NW) A 18 a 8.7.	24 "		Battalion marched to Cardoen Farm – moving off at 11am and reaching new Billets at 2pm.	
	25 "		A.B. and half of C Coy parading inner Coy arrangements. C Coy provided working parties under R.Es. D Coy moves to VOX VRIE FM for work under Commandant 38th Divn. Inspection of Box Respirators and PH helmets by Divisional Gas Officer.	

WAR DIARY or INTELLIGENCE SUMMARY

17th Royal Welsh Fusiliers

Place	Date 1917	Hour	Summary of Events and Information	Remarks and references to Appendices
CARDOEN FARM A.18.a.8.7.	May 26		Parade a.m. Coy arrangements for Training. Working parties supplied as before. Baths at Elverdinghe.	
	27		Sunday - Church parade. All demonstration - lewis working parties. Gas Alarm at 3 am Battalion turned out and all precautions taken.	
	28		Alarm proved to be false. Working parties and training as before. Two officers to Gervais and T.M. Course at TERDEGHEM.	
	29		Capt R. Lloyd Williams returned from Adjutants Course. Working parties and training.	
	30		All Coys employed on Working parties. Capt H.Q. employed men paraded for training at 11 am and 2 pm. Capt R.Lloyd Williams to ARRAS for tank demonstration. Sergt [?] Jones awarded MEDAILLE MILITAIRE.	
	31		All Coys on Working parties. Capt H.Q. employed men training as above.	

H Stanley
Lieut Col
Commdg 17 RW Fus

Army Form C. 2118.

WAR DIARY
or
INTELLIGENCE SUMMARY

17th Bttn Royal Welsh Fusiliers

(Erase heading not required.)

Instructions regarding War Diaries and Intelligence Summaries are contained in F. S. Regs., Part II. and the Staff Manual respectively. Title Pages will be prepared in manuscript.

Place	Date	Hour	Summary of Events and Information	Remarks and references to Appendices
CARDOEN FARM A18 a 8.7.	June 1st 1917		Battalion at CARDOEN FARM with 1 Company at YOX VRIE FARM. Working Parties supplied for Cable Burying under R.E. Signals, work on Prisoners Cages & usual supervision of M.M.P.	
	2nd		Working parties supplied as previous day with training for Coy employed men at 11am & 2pm. Inadequate employed men on Bombing practice under Sergt Salt. 2/Lieut Atseal on leave. 1 O.R. wounded.	
	3rd		Working parties supplied as previous day. Religious services for all denominations from Brigade. Battalion Stood to and all necessary precautions taken.	
	4th		Usual working parties and training. — ditto —	
CARDOEN FARM A18 a 6.7	5th		— ditto — — ditto —	

2449 Wt. W14957/M90 750,000 1/16 J.B.C. & A. Forms/C.2118/12.

WAR DIARY
or
INTELLIGENCE SUMMARY

Army Form C. 2118.

17th Royal Welsh Fusiliers

Place	Date	Hour	Summary of Events and Information	Remarks and references to Appendices
CARDOEN FARM A 18.a.8.7.	June 1917 6		Working parties on Cable Burying and Infantry track making. Instruments, reviews and Fife and Drum Band formed.	
	7		Working parties and training.	
	8		Working parties and training, night patrols independent for one night. Lieut. G.R. Strokes on leave.	
	9		Working parties and training. Boxing tournaments held in the evening.	
	10		Services of all denominations. Coy E served at Roussell Farm. Working parties as usual. Finals of the Boxing held at night. 2/Lieut. S. Phillips and D.J. Richards returned from France and S.T. Courses.	
	11		Working parties and training. 2/Lieut. J.B. Hartley on leave. Operation Orders received from Brigade and issued this day. New Class Patrol "D"	

Army Form C. 2118.

WAR DIARY
or
INTELLIGENCE SUMMARY

17th Batt. Royal Welsh Fusiliers

(Erase heading not required.)

Place	Date	Hour	Summary of Events and Information	Remarks and references to Appendices
CARDOEN FARM A18 & 7.	June 1917 11th		Commanders Course commenced under Major Kelly. The following Officers attended - 2/Lieut B Rees and 2/Lieut M.G.R.Morgan.	
	12th		Working parties and Training up to 12 noon only. During the afternoon preparations made for moving. 9.30pm Battalion moved from CARDOEN FARM into the BLEUET FARM area. Dispositions of Coys as follows - A Coy BARN FARM, B Coy PARADOU FARM, C Coy Right Coy X Lines, D Coy Left Coy X Lines. Bn HQ at BLEUET FARM. Relief complete reported to Bde HQ about 12 midnight.	
BLEUET FM. B10 c.3.3.	13th		Working parties supplied from 12 noon. Slight training carried on in vicinity of Billets. 2/Lieut J Roberts joined the Battalion for duty and posted to A Coy 2/Lieut A.P. Searle returned from leave.	
BLEUET FARM B10 c.3.3.	14th		Working parties supplied and general maintenance of trenches. Operation Orders	

Army Form C. 2118.

WAR DIARY
or
INTELLIGENCE SUMMARY 17th Royal Welsh Fusiliers
(Erase heading not required.)

Place	Date	Hour	Summary of Events and Information	Remarks and references to Appendices
BLEUET FARM. B10 C.3.3.	June 14. 1917		received. Battalion moved from BLEUET FARM into the X line extension, having being relieved by the 1st Bn Scots Guards. Relief complete reported at 1.20 a.m.	
X. LINE EXTENSION	15.		Battalion Headquarters at Wood west of TRAM CAR COT. B.17 a+c. A Coy B.17 a+c B Coy B.17 C.1.4. C+D Coys 'X' line extension. Working parties engaged on Cable Burying on CANAL BANK also Camouflaging on new Lt Tracks.	
	16.		2/Lieut James Ellis joined the Battalion for duty and posted to 'D Coy. 6 ORs wounded. Companies engaged on Cable Burying and Camouflaging. Work greatly impeded owing to intense hostile shelling.	
X LINE EXTENSION	17th		Working parties etc as previous night. 1 OR killed + 2 OR wounded. Lieut Col A. Taylor on leave. 2/Lieut Ja Shone on leave. 2/Lieut J.P. Williams on specine. Course of Bayonet Fighting at ST POL.	

WAR DIARY or INTELLIGENCE SUMMARY

Army Form C. 2118.

17th Batt. Royal Welsh Fusiliers

Place	Date 1917	Hour	Summary of Events and Information	Remarks and references to Appendices
'X' LINE EXTENSION	June 18th		Working parties etc as previous night. Brigade Signalling Class assembled at VOX VRIE (A15b 4.5). 3 O.Rs wounded. Sergt Stanley proc. to UK for Commission.	
			15 O.Rs from Rest Camp AMBLETEUSE. During the afternoon several shells were dropped in the vicinity of Battalion Headquarters.	
	19th		Working parties etc as previous night. 2/Lieut H.G.R Morgan to Platoon Commanders Course at PROVEN. 2/Lieut B Rees to HAZEBROUCK for interview with R.F.C.	
	20th		Working parties as usual. 2/Lieut OB Rees returned from HAZEBROUCK and proceeded to PROVEN to join Platoon Commanders Course. Sergt M Williams to UK for Commission.	
'X' LINE EXTENSION	21st		Working parties on Cable Burying, Camouflaging etc. 1 O.R killed 5 O.R wounded.	

Army Form C. 2118.

WAR DIARY
or
INTELLIGENCE SUMMARY

(Erase heading not required.)

17th Battn Royal Welsh Fusiliers

Place	Date	Hour	Summary of Events and Information	Remarks and references to Appendices
"X" LINE EXTENSION	1917 21st		32 Reinforcements joined the Battn and posted to Companies.	
	22nd		Cable Burying parties cancelled. Coys employed in "X" line extension.	
	23rd		Capt D P Oliver to NOYELLES. Heavy shelling with 4.2 and 5.9 in wood.	
			Bn S.R. (Bn. 9.c.) about 150 rounds fired. Road evacuated and new	
			Bn H.Q. made at B 19 c 4. 3½. 2 Officers and 9 O.R. wounded. C.S.M. P. Banwell wounded	
	24th		10 p.m. vicinity of New Bn HQ was shelled by small calibre guns. Out of	
			100 rounds, 80 shrowin were counted – apparently light armour piercing shells.	
	25th		At 3 am vicinity of Bn H.Q. again shelled by same calibre guns. About	
			60 to 70% were "duds".	
	26th		Operation Orders received and issued. Preparations made for moving from the	
			"X" line extension. 1 OR wounded.	
	27th		At 1 am Battalion moved from the "X" line and proceeded to ELVERDINGHE	

WAR DIARY
or
INTELLIGENCE SUMMARY

(Erase heading not required.)

Army Form C. 2118.

17th Bn Royal Welsh Fusiliers

Place	Date 1917	Hour	Summary of Events and Information	Remarks and references to Appendices
PROVEN F.7.b.1.2.	27th		From where it marched along the Railway track to INTERNATIONAL CORNER, thence by tram to PROVEN arriving at about 5.45 a.m.	
CAESTRE P.36.b.	28th		Held PROVEN, and breakfast was served at 6.45 a.m. At about 8.30 a.m. the Battalion entrained from PROVEN and proceeded to CAESTRE (about P.36.b. S.7, sheet 27). 18 Reinforcements join Battalion. The B attalion left the CAESTRE area at 8.15 a.m. and proceeded by Bus via HAZEBROUCK, MORBECQUE, STEENBECQUE, BOESEGHEM, AIRE, LAMBRES, ST HILLAIRE, WESTREHEM to PALFART, arriving at 12.40 p.m. Coys reported complete in Billets at 1.30 p.m. 2/Lieut J Roberts & 2/Lt J Ellis proceeded to Platoon Commanders Course at XIV Corps School BOLLEZEELE. 2/Lieut R Stock present to the above School on L.G. Course.	
PALFART	29th		Morning devoted to cleaning up. Kit inspections held and lists of all deficiencies made out to Orderly Room. Inspection of Arms by Corps are By HQ. F.G.C.M. held at Bn H.Q. to trial of Pte Sanny & Pte Bruno. 2/Lieut J.A. Shone returned from leave.	
	30th		Platoon Training in all Coys. no movements. The new draft paraded under to R.S.M. at 7 a.m. All Regimental & Coy Signallers given skeleton instruction under the direction of Sergt Wills (Regimental Sergt).	

M J Taylor Lieut Col.
Commanding 17 RWF

SECRET. Copy.No.

OPERATION ORDERS.No.29.
BY LIEUT COL H.J.TAYLOR.
COMMANDING 17th&6BATTALION ROYAL WELSH FUSILIERS.

1. The Battalion will relieve the 16th Batt Welsh Regiment in the SUPPORT AREA tomorrow night.
2. Dispositions of Companies will be as follows :-
    "X" LINE -RIGHT"C" Coy.
    "X" LINE -LEFT."D" "
    PARADOU FARM. "B" "
    BARN FARM.   "A" "
3. Battalion will not move forward of ELVERDINGHE before 10.p.m. The usual precautions will be taken, and Traffic Regulations strictly complied with.
4. Companies will move off in the above order, preceded by Batt H.Q., at 9:25.p.m. 200 yards distance to be maintained between Platoons. Route will be as follows :-
    Infantry Track No.10 as far as Dressing Station, thence along road past Barn and Paradou Farms, Bridge Street. Unless the roads are being shelled, X LINE Companies will proceed from ELEGEM along Trolley Line, and along road to White Hope Corner. Right, and Left, respectively.
5. Lewis Gunners and Signallers will relieve under arrangements made by their respective Officers. X LINE Lewis Gunners and Signallers will move immediately in front of their Companies.
6. All Trench Stores, Defence Scheme, Details of Work, and all information regarding the Area, will be taken over and receipts passed, copies of which will be rendered to Orderly Room in duplicate by 9.a.m. 13th. instant.
7. Companies in X LINE will render a certificate to Orderly Room by 9.a.m. 13th instant, that all ranks know the positions to be occupied in the X LINE, South of the Railway.
8. Orders re Stores and Trench Kit etc, will be issued later.
9. Relief complete will be reported to Battalion Headquarters by RUNNER.

ACKNOWLEDGE.   (signed) R. Lloyd Williams. Capt.
Issued at 6.p.m.   Actg Adjt.
11th. June. 1917.

Copy No.1. War Diary.   Copy No. 6. O.C."B" Coy.
        2. File.   7. O.C."C" "
        3. 16th.Welsh Regt.   8. O.C."D" "
        4. 11th.S.W.B.   9. O.H and T.C.
        5. O.C."A" Coy.   10. R.S.M.
              11. Signalling Officer.

Headquarters.
115 Inf. Bde.

Herewith Original Copy of War Diary of this Unit for July 1917.

C.H. Edwards, Major
O.C. 17 R.W.F.

WAR DIARY or INTELLIGENCE SUMMARY

Army Form C. 2118.

17th Battalion Royal Welch Fusiliers

Vol 20

Place	Date 1917	Hour	Summary of Events and Information	Remarks and references to Appendices
PALFART (Fibre).	July 1st		Sunday - Services for all denominations.	
	" 2nd		Training in accordance with Brigade programme in the Training Area from 9 am to 4 pm. Draft of 28 Other Ranks joined the Battalion. Capt J.R.Dale on leave.	
	3rd		Battalion employed on Trench digging etc in the Training Area	
	4th		Training in the Training Area from 9 am to 8.30 pm. 3 G.C.M. in the case of 4 ch Sexcy 'B' coy. Held at Battalion HQ.	
	5th		Battalion training in the Training ground, and bivouaced in the Training ground ready to commence training the following morning at 3 am.	
			48 OR (draft) joined the Battalion and the training was under the supervision of the R.S.M. 57105 Pte Ernest Williams, a private of the unit, awarded the Military Medal for bravery in the field.	
	6th		Battalion training in Training Area; Bivouac Bay. 4 OR on leave.	

Army Form C. 2118.

WAR DIARY
or
INTELLIGENCE SUMMARY
(Erase heading not required.)

17th Bn Royal Welsh Fusiliers

Instructions regarding War Diaries and Intelligence Summaries are contained in F. S. Regs., Part II. and the Staff Manual respectively. Title Pages will be prepared in manuscript.

Place	Date	Hour	Summary of Events and Information	Remarks and references to Appendices
PALFART (Fovin)	July 1917 7.		Battalions training on Training area. 2/Lieut O'Relan & 2/Lt R. Lebeau	
	8.		Training at disposal of Company Commanders. Carried on Battalion Training field from 9.30 to 11 am. Church Service celebrated	
	9.		Holy Communion for all denominations. Lecture delivered by the Divisional Gas Officer on the use of the Box Respirator & P.H. helmet" to the last 3 drafts.	
	10.		Battalion training under Coy arrangements on Bn Training field	
	11.		Battalion training on Training Area	
			— do —	
	12.		Divisional Day- Training in accordance with Divine Programme. Battalion bivouaced at night on Training Area.	

Army Form C. 2118.

WAR DIARY
or
INTELLIGENCE SUMMARY

(Erase heading not required.)

17th Bn Royal Welsh Fusiliers

Place	Date 1917	Hour	Summary of Events and Information	Remarks and references to Appendices
PALFART (Febrin)	July 13.		Battalion returned to Billets from Training ground at 11a.m. Rest of day	
	14.		devoted to sleep.	
	15.		Battalion allotted Range in Training Area. 4 O.R. proceeded on leave. 2/Lieut Palek to R.F.C. for duty. 2/Lieut C.A. Seal admitted to Hospital.	
			Camp Frost to XIN Corps School as Sergeant Major	
MOLINGHEM	16.		Battalion left PALFART and marched to Billets at MOLLINGHEM	
CAESTRA	17		Battalion left MOLINGHEM for the CAESTRA area arriving about 3pm	
ECKE.	18		Battalion left CAESTRA area and marched to billets in the ECKE area.	
PROVEN.	19.		Battalion left ECKE area and marched to a camp in the vicinity of PROVEN.	
SEATON CAMP (F.5.d.4.1.)	20.	3.45 pm	Battalion marched from PROVEN to SEATON CAMP (F.5.d.4.1.).	

WAR DIARY or INTELLIGENCE SUMMARY

Army Form C. 2118.

17th Bn Royal Welsh Fusiliers

Place	Date	Hour	Summary of Events and Information	Remarks and references to Appendices
SEATON CAMP (F.5.d.4.1.)	July 1917 21st		Parades held under Coy arrangements for the training of specialists. Kit and Gasbelmet inspection. Capt J. Sheriff-Roberts proceeds to 9 Squadron R.F.C. for course in Aircraft Observation. Working party of 200 OR supplied for work on PARRDY FARM (Cable Burying).	
	22nd		Church parades for all denominations. 2/Lieut Wennington rejoined from leave, having been granted 13 days extension by War Office.	
	23rd		Specialist training, and handling of platoons under Coy arrangements. YUKON PACK demonstration. Inspection of Battalion Fighting Kit by G.O.C.	
	24th		Training under Coy arrangements.	
SEATON CAMP (F.5.d.4.1.)	25		- do - . Demonstrating & firing of a Rifle grenade flare. Baths for the whole Battalion near International Corner.	

Army Form C. 2118.

WAR DIARY
or
INTELLIGENCE SUMMARY

(Erase heading not required.)

17th Royal Welsh Fusiliers

Place	Date	Hour	Summary of Events and Information	Remarks and references to Appendices
SEATON CAMP. (F.S.d.u.1.)	July 1917 26.		Training under Coy arrangements. Training for Specialists. Inspection of Gasmasks and Gas drill.	
	27th		Physical Exercise, Gas drill, and Practical handling of Platoon. Preliminary notes re ewes to move within 1 hour. Battalion ready to move at 6 p.m.	
	28th		Training in Musketry and Lewis Gun instruction. Bayonet Drill etc. Men resting during the afternoon. Lectures delivered in the Evening by the Platoon Commanders to the men. 2/Lieuts. J.Roberts and J.Ellis returned from courses at BOLLEZEELE.	
	29th		Sunday. Services for all denominations. Operation Orders received. Battalion moved from SEATON CAMP at 9.45 p.m. and proceeded to "H" Camp (AQ28.7.) Battalion reported present in billets at 2 a.m. 30/7/17.	
	30th		Draft of 19 O.R. joined the Battalion. Reconnaissance of new tracks carried out	

Army Form C. 2118.

WAR DIARY
or
INTELLIGENCE SUMMARY

(Erase heading not required.) 17th Bn Royal Welsh Fusiliers

Place	Date	Hour	Summary of Events and Information	Remarks and references to Appendices
"H" Camp (A9c8.7)	July 30. 1917		by Officers of the Battalion and preparations made for evacuating the Camp. The Battalion left "H" Camp at 9 p.m. and moved forward to the "X" line. Details and Transport encamped at Transport lines about A10d.	
	31st	3.50	Battalion left the assembly trenches at "zero plus 1 hour" viz 4.50 with C Coy on the right directing and D Coy on its left in the leading waves. B Coy in support and A Coy as carriers moving in rear. Objective STEENBEEK own Guns dotted line, Barrage right & left – 114 Inf. Bde & 113 Inf. Bde respectively. Casualties not ascertained.	

C.H. Edwards
Major
OC 17. RWF

WAR DIARY or INTELLIGENCE SUMMARY

(Erase heading not required.)

17th BATTALION Royal Welsh Fusiliers

Place	Date 1917	Hour	Summary of Events and Information	Remarks and references to Appendices
STEENBEEK.	August 1		Battalion in the STEENBEEK. Casualties 324 Other Ranks and 16 Officers	
	2nd		Officer in Command 2/Lieut J.J. Williams. Battalion relieved in the line night of the 2nd by part of 15 H.L.I. Battalion came down to CANAL BANK. All details from Transport lines marched up to CANAL BANK. 2nd in Command (Major T.R.Evans) to assume	
CANAL BANK B24 b.			the reorganisation of the Battalion. Lieut Col C.C. Edwards in Command.	
	3		Working party employed (20 Officers 400 OR). Men rested during the morning.	
	4		Men had rest & sleep. Special precautions taken against enemy form of Frightfulness	
			by continuous shell shelling & care generally of the feet. 2/Lieut J. Ellis got OR	
			to 5th Army School of Instruction.	
	5th		Battalion relieved on Canal Bank by a limit of the 20th (Light) Divisioners	

WAR DIARY or INTELLIGENCE SUMMARY

Army Form C. 2118.

17th BATTALION Royal Welsh Fusiliers

Place	Date 1917	Hour	Summary of Events and Information	Remarks and references to Appendices
ELVERDINGHE	Aug 5		Marched down to ELVERDINGHE grounds were a hot meal was provided. In the afternoon a bath was given the men and after this the Battalion marched to the Railway Siding at Elverdinghe and entrained for ST SIXTE, marching hence to SEATON CAMP (F&C 4.6.)	
SEATON CAMP (F&C 4.6)	6		Day devoted to cleaning up etc. Coys at disposal of Coy Commanders.	
	7		Inspection of Kit etc. Indents to QM. also indents for Mobilisation Stores.	
	8		Men allowed 24 hours Rest and Sleep in accordance with Divisional Circular letter. Superintendant of Bayonet Fighting lectured to the Officers & NCOs at B.H.Q. Officer arrived rejoined the Battalion from Hospital.	
	9		Inspection of Battalion by G.O.C. at 9 a.m. on Battalion Parade ground. Instruction in Section Training Given also Platoon Drill carried on. Physical Training	

WAR DIARY or INTELLIGENCE SUMMARY

Army Form C. 2118.

Place	Date 1917	Hour	Summary of Events and Information	Remarks and references to Appendices
SEATON CAMP. (F5c 4 b)	Aug 9th		Bayonet Fighting & Musketry.	
	10th		2/Lieut S J Phillips and 1 NCO to Musketry Course at TOUTENCOURT. Battalion on the Range. Musketry, Fire Discipline; Control & Manual training. Platoon in attack. Simple tactical Scheme for Officers & NCOs.	
	11th		Bombing ground allotted to the Battalion. Special Physical Training Refresher Class in use as CSM force (SNB). Bombing, Rifle Grenade Practice, Bayonet Fighting. at Baths at Contrare Chateau allotted to the Unit.	
	12th		Sunday: Ceremonial Parade; Church Services for all Denominations.	
	13th		Recreational Games. Gas Drill, Lewis Gun drill, Fire Control & Physical training.	
			P.T. Class under CSM Jones.	
	14th		Rifle Range allotted to the Battalion. Spec P.T. class under CSM Jones. Battalion.	

Army Form C. 2118.

WAR DIARY
or
INTELLIGENCE SUMMARY.
(Erase heading not required.)

Place	Date	Hour	Summary of Events and Information	Remarks and references to Appendices
SEATON CAMP (F.S.C.4.6)	1917 Aug: 14		Ceremonial Parade. Battalion in formation for the attack. Gas Drill etc.	
	15		Class P. Training under O.S.M. Jones. Musketry Tactical Scheme. Hygiene Drills	
	16		Bayonet Fighting.	
			Rifle Range allotted to Battalion. Training under Coy arrangements.	
			Military Medals awarded to the following NCO's men:- 2931 CQMS Williams R.T., 3917 L/Cpl Davies H, 26152 Cpl Williams J, 27854 Pte Hall T.O., 25271 Pte Jones S.H. 55915 Pte Thomas J.N. Battn at Cortons allotted limit.	
	17		Parades under Coy Arrangements. Lecture for NCO's by the C.O. 1/ Sergt R. 2SOR to 151 Coy R.E. for attachment. 2/Lieut W. Pennington accompanied by 4 Battalion Runners proceeded to Canal Bank to take Over.	
	18		Details of HERZEELE proceeded at 9 am and march to HERZEELE.	

Army Form C. 2118.

WAR DIARY
or
INTELLIGENCE SUMMARY.
(Erase heading not required.)

Place	Date 1917	Hour	Summary of Events and Information	Remarks and references to Appendices
SEATON. CAMP. F5C.4.b.	Aug 18		All Officers & Other Ranks for 1st line paraded at 11.30 and marched to CANAL BANK. Details for 'H' Camp paraded at 1pm and marched from Seaton Camp to 'H' Camp. (A9C.8.7.)	
H Camp. A9C.8.7.	19		Sunday – Services for all Denominations held at H' Camp.	
	20		Parades from 9am to 12 noon & 2pm to 4pm shall include Physical Training, Bayonet Fighting & Close Order Drill. 2 OR to Regimeres Course at Esquelbecq.	
	21		Parades as previous day also Gas helmet drill. 2/Lieut B Rees & OR proceed on Course to XIV Corps School. Football Match held in the afternoon. Following Decorations awarded – Military Cross – Lieut J.L. Williams, 2/Lieut J.B. Hartly. 2/Lieut S.J. Phillips. D.C.M – Sergt R. Priests and Cpl R.O. Davies all of this Unit.	
	22		Parades as previous day, PT & BF Class, Close Order Drill, Musketry firing on the Range. Sports held in the afternoon.	

WAR DIARY or INTELLIGENCE SUMMARY

Army Form C. 2118.

17th BATTALION Royal Welsh Fusiliers

Place	Date 1917	Hour	Summary of Events and Information	Remarks and references to Appendices
"H" Camp Aq&7.	Aug 23.		Carried on previous Day. 1 O.R. for Musketry Instructors course at GHQ School (Rifle Brigade) CAMIERS. Divisional Baths allotted. Details from 2.30 to 4 pm. 2/Lieut G Ellis + 15 O.R. wounded in line.	
	24.		Parades in morning as follows - Close Order Drill, Musketry, Shooting on the Range. Afternoon devoted to Recreational Training & games. The following reinforcements arrived - 2/Lieut J Gleckie + 86 O.R.	
	25.		Day devoted to cleaning up & making up deficiencies in kit etc.	
	26.		Sunday. Religious Services for all denominations. 2/Lieut R) Baird arrived as reinforcement. 9 O.R. wounded in the line. Bath at 7am.	
	27.		Parades - Musketry, Physical Drill, Bayonet Fighting. 2o in Command left "H" Camp to take Command of 15 Battalion. Lieut Cue C. Edwards wounded.	
	28.		Training at "H" Camp as usual. 25 O.Ranks arrived as Reinforcement	

WAR DIARY or INTELLIGENCE SUMMARY

Army Form C. 2118.

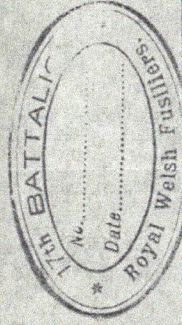

17th BATTALION Royal Welsh Fusiliers

Place	Date	Hour	Summary of Events and Information	Remarks and references to Appendices
"H" Camp	1917 Aug. 28		Casualties: 1 Officer killed, 2 Officers wounded, 6 OR killed & 130 OR wounded.	
	29.		Details Training no scheme at 'H' Camp. Battalion was relieved in the line & came down to HULLS FARM (B.18.c.9.t.).	
	30.		Training at 'H' Camp which included Musketry, Bayonet Fighting, Physical Drill, Close Order Drill & Gas helmet drill.	
	31.		Battalion moved from Hulls Farm to L.2. Usual Training Carried on at H Camp	

E. O. Shuffleton Captain
for O.C. 17 R.W.Fus

Army Form C. 2118.

WAR DIARY
or
INTELLIGENCE SUMMARY.
(Erase heading not required.)

Place	Date 1917	Hour	Summary of Events and Information	Remarks and references to Appendices
MALAKOFF CAMP B.22.b.1. (St Julien)	Sept 1st		Battalion at MALAKOFF CAMP. Training under Company arrangements.	
	2nd		— do —	
	3rd		— do —	
	4th		The G.O.C. presented Military Cross & Military Medal Ribbons to Officers & OR of this Unit. Battalion relieved by 16th R.W.Fusiliers at Malakoff Camp and proceeded to	
CANDLE CANCER TRENCH (C.8 & 28.)			relieve the 13th B. Welsh Regt in CANDLE – CANCER TRENCH. (C.8 & 28 Belgium 28NW). Relief Complete by 11pm. Casualties 1 OR wounded.	
	5th		Battalion in support area CANDLE – CANCER TRENCH. 2 OR proceeded on leave. Casualties 1 OR wounded.	
	6th		Battalion in support area.	
	7th		Battalion in support area. Casualties 5 OR wounded.	
	8th		Battalion in support area. 1 OR proceeded on leave.	

Army Form C. 2118.

WAR DIARY
or
INTELLIGENCE SUMMARY.
(Erase heading not required.)

Instructions regarding War Diaries and Intelligence Summaries are contained in F. S. Regs., Part II. and the Staff Manual respectively. Title pages will be prepared in manuscript.

Place	Date	Hour	Summary of Events and Information	Remarks and references to Appendices
CANDLE – CANCER TRENCH.	1917 Sept. 9.		Battalion relieved in Support by 1/5 7th D.C.L.I. Relief Complete by about 2 p.m. After relief, Battalion marched to ELVERDINGHE where it entrained for PROVEN.	
PALMA CAMP	10th		Battalion took over new PALMA CAMP and reported present in Billets by 7 p.m. Major C/t Edwards rejoined the Battalion from Hospital.	
	11th		Battalion at PALMA CAMP. Battn. allotted to 1st Battalion at COUTHOVE CHATEAU. Remainder of the day devoted to Medical & Kit inspections. 7 Officers arrived as reinforcements.	
			Battalion at PALMA CAMP. Training under Coy arrangements.	
EECKE.	12th		Battalion marched to EECKE and arrived in Billets by 12 noon.	
MORBECQUE	13th		Battalion marched to MORBECQUE and occupied Billets in the Village. Major Edwards evacuated to Hospital.	
SAILLY SUR-LA-LYS G 22.b.2.8 MAP 36.	14th		Battalion marched from MORBECQUE to SAILLY-SUR-LA-LYS and arrived in Billets about 6 p.m. Lieut. QM J ff Jones proceeded on leave.	

WAR DIARY of INTELLIGENCE SUMMARY

Army Form C. 2118.

Place	Date 1917	Hour	Summary of Events and Information	Remarks and references to Appendices
ARMENTIERES SECTOR	Sept. 15		The Battalion marched to the Reserve Billets at ARMENTIERES doctors, relieving the 2/5th Bn. K.O.R.L. Regt. (57th Division). Relief complete by 11.30 p.m. Disposition in Reserve Area as follows — "A" "B" Coys in the subsidiary line ("C" & "D" Coys in the JUTE FACTORY (B.29 r b.3). Battalion H.Q. at H.5.t.80.65.	
	16		Battalion in Reserve. Training under Company arrangements.	
	17		Battalion in Reserve. Training & inspection of kit at Working Parties supplies.	
	18		Battalion in Reserve. Training & inspection of Kit. Hygiene inspection. Major C/t. Edwards returned from hospital 17/9/17.	
	19		Battalion in Reserve. Major C/t. Edwards proceeded on leave 19/9/17.	
	20		2/Lieut Phillips returned from 5th Army School of Instruction. 5 O.R. on leave. 1 wounded	
	21		Battalion in Reserve. 5 O.R. on leave. 4 men attached to 115 T.M.B.	
	22		Battalion in Reserve. 3 O.R. proceeded on Signalling Course.	
	23		1 O.R. to Signal Course at DUNSTABLE. The Battalion relieved the 16th Welsh	

WAR DIARY or INTELLIGENCE SUMMARY.

Army Form C. 2118.

17th BATTALION Royal Welsh Fusiliers

Place	Date	Hour	Summary of Events and Information	Remarks and references to Appendices
HOUPLINES SUB-SECTOR	Sept 1917 23rd		Regt: in the Houplines sector. disposition in the line as follows:- A Coy Right, B Coy left, C Coy centre, D Coy support. B.H.Q at C.28.a.7.8.	
	24th		Battalion in Line. Reconnoitering & working parties out. 2/Lieut Phillips on leave. 1 OR Killed 2 OR wounded	
	25.		" " 2/Lieut EW Griffith & 5 OR to Sniping Coy. Capt Alt Sead proceeded on leave. 39 Reinfor came to join the Unit.	
	26.		Battalion in line. Working parties employed on cleaning & improving trenches. Q.M. in line. 2 OR Killed 3 OR wounded.	
	27.		Battalion in the line. Work being carried out in trench lines. Officer O.T. [?] joins. Casualties 2 OR Killed & 3 OR wounded	
	28.		to Batt: for duty. Battalion in the line. Work etc as usual. 2/Lt Griffith to Sniping Course. 10 Reinforcements arrived.	
	29.		Battalion in line. 1 Officer 1 OR rejoins 1 OR recourses 5 Oth Ranks joins as Reinforcements to work as usual.	
	30.		Battalion in line. 1 Platoon H (Officers & 40 OR) relieved at 11am by 16 Welsh. The former proceeded to Brigade School (H5a & 7). 2/Lieut F Roberts & 1 OR wounded.	

J. B. Cochran Lieut Col
Commanding 17 R.W.Fus:

WAR DIARY
or
INTELLIGENCE SUMMARY.

Army Form C. 2118.

No. 1.

17 RWF

22ⁿᵈ G.

2ⁿᵈ R.W.F. Bn 30 NW & Houplines.

Place	Date 1917	Hour	Summary of Events and Information	Remarks and references to Appendices
HOUPLINES Sub-Sector.	Oct 1ˢᵗ		Battalion relieved in Houplines sub-sector on night 1/2 October by 16ᵗʰ Welsh Regt. O. & D. Coys. trained in subsidiary line – as Left & Right garrison Coys respectively. A. & B. Coys moved to Jute Factory Bog A.5.9. Battalion H.Q. at Ho.b.9.8. 2/Lt Roberts wounded.	
ARMENTIERES AREA.	2ⁿᵈ		2/Lieut. W. Pinnett joined for duty. 2/Lieut. S.P. Roberts to Divisional Depot Battalion SPILL as Adjutant & Quartermaster. Bath allotted the Battalion at "Laundries". 2 O.R. wounded. Washing parties supplied in R.E. work and Cable burying to about at 7.30 p.m. Rifle, kit & equipment inspections held in the morning. Lectures delivered	
		3ᵖᵐ	in the afternoon by O.C. Coys which included the reading of. to army acts etc. Washing parties supplied as before on day.	
		4ᵉ	2/Lieut's Carter & Lord joined the Bn as Reinforcements. 2 ORs sent as guides for Bn HQ & D Coys C.E.P. Coy arrangements. 3 NCOs sent as guides for Bn HQ & D Coys C.E.P. (Pithgear) from 16ᵗʰ Bde H.Q. to Jute Factory. "C" Coy C.E.P. attached to the unit.	

Army Form C. 2118.

WAR DIARY
or
INTELLIGENCE SUMMARY.
(Erase heading not required.)

Place	Date	Hour	Summary of Events and Information	Remarks and references to Appendices
ARMENTIERES AREA.	Oct. 4th 1917	5pm	2/Lieut. J. Jones joined the Battalion as reinforcement. Range allotted this Unit from 8am to 1pm and used by A+B Coys and Lewis Gunners. Following Officers joined as Reinforcements. Major W.A.Whitton, 2/Lieut. J.H.Roach and 2/Lieut. D.H.Jennings. Working parties supplied. Capt. L.P.Crane. R.A.M.C. wounded by bomb from hostile aircraft.	
	6th		Classes under Coy arrangements in Lewis Gun, Musketry, Fire Control and Training and Lewis Gun instruction. Concert held in the evening at Jute Factory and attended by G.O.C. Working parties supplied: time of reporting prolonged by special permission from Bde. Battalion relieved 16th Welsh Regt. in Houplines sub-sector 7/8th October. Relieving front line. B Coy. left, C Coy. Centre. D Coy. right.	
HOUPLINES SUB-SECTOR	7th		4 Coys in the line as follows:—	

WAR DIARY or INTELLIGENCE SUMMARY

Army Form C. 2118.

Place	Date	Hour	Summary of Events and Information	Remarks and references to Appendices
HOUPLINES SUB-SECTOR.	Oct 1917 7		Support line. B. Coy. The "C" Coy C.E.P attached to the Bn. for instructional purposes. Relief complete about 1.15 am 8/10/1917. 1 O.R wounded.	
	8		Battalion in the line. Working parties employed for work in subsidiary line. 2/Lieut S.T.O.Riddiko rejoined from leave. 2 O.R killed.	
	9		Battalion in the line. Working parties employed for H.T.M. emplacements and R.E work in the subsidiary line. 1 O.R for Lewis Gun School Le Touquet.	
	10		4 O.R wounded. 4 N.C.O's sent on Anti gas Course to SAILLY.	
			Working parties employed under R.E. on T.M Officer. Capt Attersaul on leave.	
	11		4 O.R. sent to Pigeon Flying Course. 1 O.R killed 4 O.R wounded.	
	12		F.G.C.M. held at Divnl. H.Q. for the trial of 23606 Pte Roberts & 23507 Pte Jones of this bn. Usual working parties employed. 5 Officers and 9 O.R on Courses. 20 R wounded.	
ARMENTIERES AREA.	13		Battalion relieved in Front line by 16 Welsh Regt. Disposition of Coys as	

WAR DIARY or INTELLIGENCE SUMMARY

Army Form C. 2118.

No. 4

Royal Welsh Fusiliers

Place	Date	Hour	Summary of Events and Information	Remarks and references to Appendices
ARMENTIERES AREA	1917 Oct 13		A Coy left Garrison Coy Imbedding line. 1 platoon B Coy + 1 platoon D Royal Garrison Coy Imbedding line. C Coy less 1 platoon + D Coy less 1 platoon at Jute Factory. C Coy 1 platoon at Cambridge stores. Bn HQ H of b 80 65. Bn reported present in Billets at 3.10am 14/10/1917.	
	14.		4 O.R. to Pigeoneers Course. Services held for all Denominations. Working parties of 103 O.R. supplied at night for R.E. work etc.	
	15.		Services under Coy arrangements including Musketry etc. Medical Inspection of Bn HQ at 10am. 1 Officer arrived as Reinforcement.	
	16.		2/Lieut H. Charson to S.O.S. Signal school (First Army). Lieut H. Penny on leave. Parades under Coy arrangements at Jute Factory. Musketry held on range at Jute Factory. Working parties supplied. 3 O.R. wounded.	
ARMENTIERES AREA	17.		Baths at "Laundries" allotted to Battalion. Services under Section to Coys	

Army Form C. 2118.

N° 5

WAR DIARY
or
INTELLIGENCE SUMMARY.
(Erase heading not required.)

Instructions regarding War Diaries and Intelligence Summaries are contained in F. S. Regs., Part II. and the Staff Manual respectively. Title pages will be prepared in manuscript.

Place	Date	Hour	Summary of Events and Information	Remarks and references to Appendices
ARMENTIERES AREA.	Oct 1917 17.		at Citè Trebuy which included Musketry, Gas blast drill, Arms drill etc.	
	18.		2/Lieut R J Williams & 4 O Ranks arrive. Parades held under Coy arrangements	
	19.		Day devoted to cleaning up billets etc prior to leaving for the line.	
HOUPLINES Sub-sector.			Battalion relieved the 16th Welsh Regt in Houplines sub sector. Disposition as follows:- C Coy right, D Coy centre, B Coy right, A Coy support. C Coy 1st Br C.E.P. attached to this Bni. 1 OR wounded.	
	20.		Battalion in Line. Working parties subdivision accordance with "work table". Landed over by relieved unit. 2 OR killed & 2 OR wounded.	
	21st		Battalion in line. Capt. I.A.Hughes from leave. Lieut R.O.Jenkins attacks to Artillery (Battery at C.19.c-3.5.) for period of 3 days. Working parties subdivision	
	22nd		Battalion in line. 4 OR on Courses. Issued Working parties.	
HOUPLINES Sub-sector.	23rd		Battalion in line. Major J.R.Evans rejoined from Brigade School	

(A7092). Wt. W12850/M1293. 75,000. 1/17. D. D. & L., Ltd. Forms/C2118/14.

WAR DIARY or INTELLIGENCE SUMMARY

Army Form C. 2118.
N° 6.

Place	Date 1917	Hour	Summary of Events and Information	Remarks and references to Appendices
HOUPLINES DEF. Sub-sector.	23.		6. O.R. to Brigade Signalling Class. Capt A.F. Steal attended Lecture at C.A. Sch. (HQ C.3.7) Lecture delivered by Lt Col Errington.	
	24.		Capt A.F. Steal for 3 days attachment to Battery (C.19 b.3.5.) (7.5 a 63.9) Lieut J.B. Hartley rejoined Batt: from leave. Lieut R.O. Cadence returned from Bty. 3 O.R wounded	
ARMENTIERES AREA. (in reserve)	25.		Battalion relieved in the line by the 16th Welsh Regt. and proceeded to Billets at Jute Factory. Relief complete by about 11.30 hrs. C Coy C.E.P also came out of the line and stayed at Factory (B30 a 7.0). C.E.P. Bn. moved out of Brigade area 27.	
	26.		1 Officer & 8 O.R. in Convoy. 5. O.R. on leave. Batt.s allotted to the Battalion. Working parties supplied as per Work Table handed in.	
	27.		Canadian Cmdn. Coy arrangemts to Capt A.F. Steal returns from Battery Special working party of 100 men plus Officers & N.C.O's employed at night	

WAR DIARY or INTELLIGENCE SUMMARY

Army Form C. 2118.

N° 7

Place	Date	Hour	Summary of Events and Information	Remarks and references to Appendices
ARMENTIERES AREA. (Reserve)	Oct 27		Carrying Stokes Mortar Bombs.	
	28.		Sunday. Religious Services held for Church of England & Nonconformists in Jute Factory. Concert held in Jute Factory at 6.30 pm.	
	29.		2 N.C.Os to Hackett Course to LINGHEM. Bath allotted from 1-2 pm	
			2 our Armourer Sergt instructed Officers of A & B Coys in the correct method of inspecting Revolvers. 1 O.R. Killed.	
	30.		Lieut. W. Pennington from leave. To the Heatherly to U.K. for Commission. Parades under Coy Arrangements. Letter of appreciation received from G.O.C. Brigade for fine work done by working party on night 27th October. 4 O.R. wounded.	
HOUPLINES SUB-SECTY.	31.		Battalion relieved 16th Welsh Regt in trenches sub sector. Dispositions of Coys. A Coy Right Front Coy, B Coy Centre Front, C Coy Support, D Coy Left Front. Relief complete reported at 11 pm	

J.B. Cockburn Lieut Col.
Commanding 9 / 17th Bn R.W. Fus

Army Form C. 2118

WAR DIARY

INTELLIGENCE SUMMARY

(Erase heading not required.)

17th BATTALION
Royal Welsh Fusiliers

Place	Date	Hour	Summary of Events and Information	Remarks and references to Appendices
HOUPLINES Sub-sector	1st Feb 1917		Battalion in line. 19 reinforcements joined Battalion. Posted to Coys. Working parties supplied.	
	2nd		1 O.R. accidentally wounded. Capt. A.P. Hughes & 30 O.R. on leave. Working parties supplied.	
	3rd		Battalion in the line.	
	4th		Battalion in the line. 2 O.R. on courses. Gas shell bombardment from 11pm till 12.30am from 1am till 1-45am. Casualties 4 slightly wounded. 3 O.R. to reinforcements. 2nd Lt. H. Brown returned from course. Battalion in the line. 2 O.R. wounded.	
	5th			
	6th		4 Officers & 8 N.C.O's attended Lewis Gun Demonstration at 113 Inf Bde. F.G.C.M. held at Rec NO for the trial of Pte Burke & Pte Smith. 1 O.R. wounded.	
ARMENTIERES AREA (Reserve)	7th		Battalion in reserve. Baths allotted to Unit. Parades under Company arrangements. 2nd Lt Baines proceeded to Corps HQ as Intelligence Officer.	

23P
5 sheets

WAR DIARY or INTELLIGENCE SUMMARY

Army Form C. 2118

Place	Date	Hour	Summary of Events and Information	Remarks and references to Appendices
ARMENTIERES AREA	8th		Parades under company arrangements. 2 O.R. wounded. 2 O.R. to Brigade on course. Special N.C.O's class under R.S.M.	
	9th		Baths allotted from 8am to 12. Parades under company arrangements. L/C.S.M. held at Bn. H.Q. for the trial of Pte Burke & Cpl Griffiths. F/G.C.M. held at Battalion H.Q. for the trial of Pte J. Le Marno. Capt Williams & 1 O.R. proceeded on course. Operation orders received.	
HOUPLINES sub-sector	10th		Battalion relieved the 16th Welsh Regt. Disposition as follows:- "B" Coy left, "A" Coy centre, "C" Coy right, "D" Coy support. Relief completed 9.15 p.m. H.Q. Col. J.B. Cockburn to assume command of 115th Inf. Bde.	
	11th		Battalion in line. 2/Lt J. Baird and 3 O.R. proceeded on leave. 2/Lt J.O. Hughes & 2/Lt P.J. Jones returned from course. 1 O.R. wounded. 2/Lt E.C.V. Williams for 3 days attachment to 121 Batt. R.F.A.	
	12th		Battalion in line. 1 Officer, 1 N.C.O. proceeded to Rollers. 1 N.C.O. to a Yorkshire & Yukon R&R course. Cpl Jones convicted on the trial of Pte B. Smith. Cpl E.A. Shipley to a F/G.C.M. assembling at 115 M.G.C. H.Q. from 8am to 8.30am. Enemy bombarded front support & vicinity cros. Gas shell bombardment 1 O.R. wounding. From 6 - 7.30 pm. 2 O.R. killed	

Army Form C. 2118.

No 3

WAR DIARY
or
INTELLIGENCE SUMMARY.
(Erase heading not required.)

17th BATTALION
Royal Watch Fusiliers

Place	Date	Hour	Summary of Events and Information	Remarks and references to Appendices
HOUPLINES SUB. SECTOR	1917 Nov 13th		Battalion in the line. 2nd Lt A.W. Atherton attended L.G.M. at Div: H.Q. in the case of 2nd Lt Jones. Corporal H.N. Roberts proceeded to the base as orderly room sergeant. 1 N.C.O. to Div: Course. Gas shell bombardment on this sector at 11-30 p.m. & 2.30 a.m. (for 10 minutes & 15 minutes respectively.) No casualties.	
	14th		Battalion in the line. 1 O.R. killed. Two candidates for commissions interviewed by G.O.C. Div. Operations orders received from Brigade. Twenty reinforcements arrived posted to Coys. Battalion in the line. Captain R.O. Jenkins & O.R. proceeded on leave. 1 O.R. wounded.	
	15th		Battalion in the line. S.O.R. proceeded to Divisional Employment Coy for transfer to England as blonghsmen. 2nd Lt R.S. Atherton attended L.G.M. at Div H.Q. for the trial of 2nd Lt Ryan &c. Meredith. Battalion relieved by the 16th Welsh Regt and proceeded to Laundry (H5a. 50.60.) of Two Coys under orders of O.C. 115th Brigade School. Relief reported complete 6 a.m. (15/9). 1 O.R. killed.	
PLMENTIERES AREA	16th		Baths allotted. Day devoted to rest cleaning up. 3 O.R. on courses.	

WAR DIARY or INTELLIGENCE SUMMARY

Army Form C. 2118.

Place	Date	Hour	Summary of Events and Information	Remarks and references to Appendices
ARMENTIERES AREA.	Nov 18th 1914		Church service for all denominations. Concert held in the evening.	
	19th		Parade under company arrangements. 1 Officer & 5 OR proceeded on leave. 2 OR wounded.	
	20th		Parade under company arrangements. 1 OR wounded.	
	21st		Parade under company arrangements. 16 signallers to B.H.Q. for instruction. Col. Maspl A.Angle, proceeded to U.K. for concussion.	
	22nd		Day devoted to cleaning up prior to proceeding to the line. Battalion relieved the 10th Welsh R. in the Houplines left sub-sector. Dispositions as follows. "A" Coy left. "C" Coy centre. "D" Coy right. "B" Coy in support. Relief complete reported at about 10pm. 4 OR joined Bn. as reinforcements.	
HOUPLINES SUB-SECTOR.	23rd		Battalion in the line. 1 OR killed. Work carried on in accordance with work programme.	
	24th		Battalion in the line. 2 Lt Lewis proceeded on leave. 1 OR killed. 1 OR wounded. Revd Pennington to Battery 121 F.A. for 3 days attachment. 1 Officer & 6 OR on leave. 2 OR wounded.	
	25th		Battalion in line. Revd Pennington to Battery 121 F.A. for 3 days attachment. 1 Officer & 6 OR on leave. 2 OR wounded.	

WAR DIARY or INTELLIGENCE SUMMARY.

Army Form C. 2118.

Place	Date	Hour	Summary of Events and Information	Remarks and references to Appendices
HOUPLINES SUB-SECTOR	1917 Feb 26th		Battalion in the line. 2 Officers & 10 O.R. proceeded on course to XI Corps School.	
	27th		Battalion in the line. 4 signallers proceeded to Brigade for training.	
	28th		Battalion relieved in the line by 16th Welsh Regt. Four Coys in Subsidiary Line, and Battalion H.Q. at H.5.c.8.6. Vigorous hostile shelling of Bn. H.Q. with 4.2 & 5.9 from 2.30pm to 3.15pm. 1 O.R. wounded	
	29th		Battalion in Subsidiary line. Bn. H.Q. at H.5.c.8.6.	
	30th		Battalion in Subsidiary line. Baths allotted at Laundry. 6 O.R. on leave.	

T.A. Evans
Major.
Commanding 17th Bn R.W. Fus.

Headquarters
115 Inf. Bde.

Herewith Original Copy of the
War Diary of this Unit for
the month of December 1917.

G. Pearl
Capt & Adjt
for OC 17 RWFus

MAP REF: Sheet 36NW Houplines

WAR DIARY or INTELLIGENCE SUMMARY N° 1.

(Erase heading not required.)

Instructions regarding War Diaries and Intelligence Summaries are contained in F. S. Regs., Part II. and the Staff Manual respectively. Title Pages will be prepared in manuscript.

Army Form C. 2118.

17th BATT
Date 31.1.1918
Royal Welsh Fusiliers

Place	Date	Hour	Summary of Events and Information	Remarks and references to Appendices
HOUPLINES Sub-sector	1917. Dec. 1.		Battalion in Subsidiary Line. Batt HQ at H.5.b.6.8. Batt's allotted for 1 hour pt Bn.HQ. One O.R. on course to First Army School of Instruction.	
	2nd.		Bn in Subsidiary Line. Working Party of 1 NCO & 12 O.R. supplies from Bn HQ for work in Subsidiary line. Capt J.A. Hughes rejoined from Signal Course.	
	3rd.		Bn in Subsidiary Line. Working Party supplied from Bn HQ for work in Subsidiary Line. Batt's allotted this Unit for 1 hour. Capt R.O. Jenkins rejoined from leave. 1 O.R. on leave. 2/Lieut E.L.J. Baines on Course.	
	4th.		Bn in Subsidiary Line. 2/Lieut W.G. Nicholas & 4 O.R. on leave. Operation Orders received & issued. Day devoted to cleaning up prior to leaving for the Line. Battalion relieves the 16th Welsh Regt: in the Front Line. Disposition of Coys as follows – Right front "B" Coy, Left front "C" Coy	

Houplines sub-sector

WAR DIARY or INTELLIGENCE SUMMARY

Army Form C. 2118.

N° 2.

Place	Date	Hour	Summary of Events and Information	Remarks and references to Appendices
Hopoutline Sub-sector	1917 Dec. 4.		Lieut. 'B' Coy. dis.to port 'A' coy. Lieut Col. J.B.Cockburn proceeds on leave.	
	5.		Battalion in front line. 21 Reinforcements joined & posted to Coys. 1 O.R. in Cause.	
	6.		Battalion in front line.	
	7.		Battalion in Front line. 2 Officers, 7 O.R. on Courses. 2/Lieut J.F.Lewis rejoined from leave. 3 O.R wounded.	
	8.		Battalion in Front line. G.O.C's Conference held at Bn.H.Q. 1 O.R killed. 38 Reinforcements joined the Battalion and posted to Coys.	
	9.		Battalion in Front line. Operation Orders received.	
Hopoutline And. sector	10.		Bn in front line. 2 O.R to signal School on Courses. 1 O.R to Rouen for transfer to U.K. as skilled ploughman. Battalion relieved by	

Army Form C. 2118.

WAR DIARY
or
INTELLIGENCE SUMMARY   No. 3
(Erase heading not required.)

Place	Date 1917	Hour	Summary of Events and Information	Remarks and references to Appendices
Saundries HSa 4.7	Dec. 10		the 16th Welsh Regt and proceeded to the 'Saundries' to Billets HSa 4.7	
	11.		Battalion in reserve. Baths allotted to the unit. 1 platoon & class of 8 N.C.O. for instruction under the Commandant 115th Bde School. Sergt Slavens to UK for Commission.	
	12.		Battalion in reserve. Parades under Coy arrangements. Working parties supplied. Lecture on 'Staff duties Q' at Houdain attended by C.O. & Q.M.	
	13.		Battalion in reserve. Parades under Coy arrangements. Sergt E Davies to UK for Commission. 1 Officer & 6 OR on leave. Baths from 2-4pm.	
	14.		Battalion in reserve. Parades under Coy arrangements.	
Saundries HSa 4.7			Scouts' Class held under 2/Lieut H Chown. Inter-Coy Football Match played	

WAR DIARY or INTELLIGENCE SUMMARY

Army Form C. 2118.

No. 4.

Place	Date 1917	Hour	Summary of Events and Information	Remarks and references to Appendices
Fauquissart	Dec. 14.		Between A & B Coys. went A coy 9 B coy 1.	
	15.		Battalion in reserve. Parades under Coy arrangements. Baths allotted to Coys. Special notes on 'Enemy Espionage' read out to all Coys on parade. Concert held at 5.30 p.m. also Boxing Tournament. Programme sustained by members of the 18th R.W.F. (London Welsh) and members of the unit. Capt P. Walton rejoined the Battalion and assumed (temporarily) the duties of 2nd in Command.	
	16.		Battalion in reserve. Church services held for all denominations. Battalion relieved to 16th Welsh Regt in the front line. Disposition of Coys as follows - Right front A Coy, Left front D Coy, Centre B Coy, support C Coy.	
Houplines Sub-sector	17.		Bn in front line. 2/Lieut Y O Hughes to UK for transfer to Tank Corps.	

WAR DIARY or INTELLIGENCE SUMMARY

Army Form C. 2118.

No. 5

Place	Date	Hour	Summary of Events and Information	Remarks and references to Appendices
Houplines Sub-sector	1917 Dec. 18.		Battalion in front line. 2 O.R. joined Bn as reinforcements.	
	19.		Battalion relieved in the line by the 36th Bn. A.I.F. and proceeded to Billets in ESTAIRES (L.30.C.). No casualties sustained during relief.	
	20.		Parades under Coy arrangements. Lieut Col J.B.Cockburn assumed temporary command of 113 Inf Bde.	
	21.		Battalion on Training area. Parades under Coy Commanders for drill etc. Signallers under Signal Officer. Inspection of Billets by G.O.C. Brigade.	
	22.		Battalion on Training area. Parades under Coy Commanders. Afternoon devoted to inter sports recreational training. 4 O.R. joined as reinforcements. 2/Lieut J.S.Laurence rejoined from Course.	
Estaires L.30.C.	23.		Baths allotted to the Battalion at SAILLY, from 10-12 noon + 2-3 p.m.	
	24.		Parades under Coy Commanders on the Training Area.	

WAR DIARY or INTELLIGENCE SUMMARY

Army Form C. 2118.

N° 6.

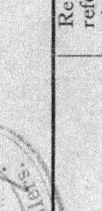

Place	Date	Hour	Summary of Events and Information	Remarks and references to Appendices
Botanire	1917 Dec. 25		Xmas Day. C of E and Nonconformist services held for the Battalion. Xmas dinners provided to the 4 Coys at 1pm and 5pm respectively. The G.O.C was present during the serving of the Dinners.	
	26.		Parades under Coy Commanders with recreational training in the Afternoon. One Coy working on the new range.	
	27.		Parades under Coy Commanders. 3 O.R. joined the Battalion.	
	28		Parades under Coy arrangements. Major J.R. Evans to 6th Bn N.Staff Regt as 2nd in Command. Capt. P. Welton assumed temporary Command of the Battalion. Pioneer to Pennington to First Army School of Instruction.	
	29.		Parades under Coy Commanders. L/Cpl Bancshaw to U.K. for Commission.	
	30		Sunday. Church Services for all Denominations. L Cpl Kendall to U.K. for Commission.	

Army Form C. 2118.

WAR DIARY
or
INTELLIGENCE SUMMARY   N° 7.
(Erase heading not required.)

Place	Date	Hour	Summary of Events and Information	Remarks and references to Appendices
Estaires	1917 Dec. 31.		Parades under Coy Commanders. Signallers detailed for training under the Signal Sergt. Lecture in the afternoon by the Corps Chemical Adviser. 2/Lieut D.K.Davies & 2/Lieut O.J.Jones to XV Corps School on Course.	

3/12/1917.

P. Welton. Capt.
Commandg; 17.Bn R.W.Ind.

WAR DIARY
or
INTELLIGENCE SUMMARY

(Erase heading not required.)

Army Form C. 2118.

No. 1.

Place	Date	Hour	Summary of Events and Information	Remarks and references to Appendices
ESTAIRES L.30.c.	Jan 1918 1st		Battalion in Estaires. Parades under Company arrangements.	S.T.P.
	2nd		Baths allotted to the Unit at SAILLY from 8–12 noon and 2–3 p.m. Lecture by G.O.C. Brigade at 130th Field Ambulance.	S.T.P.
	3rd		Parades and Training carried out under Coy arrangements.	
			Cpl Smalley to U.K. for Commission.	S.T.P.
	4th		Parade under Coy arrangements.	S.T.P.
	5th		Parades under Coy arrangements.	S.T.P.
	6th		Battalion formed up on La Petit Square Estaires at 8.45 a.m. and marched off at 8.55 a.m. for DOULIEU, arriving at Billets, at the latter place, about 10.30 a.m. Transport at 14.b.90.25.	S.T.P.
DOULIEU F.20.d.53.30.	7th		Training carried on by Coys with recreational training in the afternoon.	S.T.P.
	8th		Training carried on by Coys. 3 Signallers on Course (Aeroplane Contact) at CHOCQUES. Cpl Bradshaw to U.K. for Commission.	S.T.P.

A.T. Phillips ?/1

Army Form C. 2118.

WAR DIARY
or
INTELLIGENCE SUMMARY   N° 2.

(Erase heading not required.)

Place	Date 1918	Hour	Summary of Events and Information	Remarks and references to Appendices
DOULIEU F29d33.30.	Jan 9th		Training under Coy Arrangements.	S.T.P.
	10		Training under Coy arrangements	S.T.P.
	11		Training under Coy arrangements. 1 O.R. to Signal Course XV Corps School	S.T.P.
	12th		Training under Coy arrangements.	S.T.P.
	13th		Battalion marched from DOULIEU at 1pm and marched to previous Billets at Estaires.	S.T.P.
ESTAIRES L.30.c.	14.		One Coy on work constructing Bullet & Bayonet Courses. Other Coys training etc. All Coy Commanders, Platoon Commanders and Platoon Sergeants reconnoitred Bridge Head Posts (Portuguese Area) in the afternoon. 1 NCO to Lewis Gun Course at LeTouquet. 5 O.R. on leave.	S.T.P.
	15		4 O.R. to Course of First Aid & Sanitation at First Army R.A.M.C. school of instruction BRUAY. F.G.C.M. held at B.H.Q. for the trial of Cpl. Evans of this unit.	S.T.P.
	16		3 Coys training. 1 Coy employed on work on the Bullet & Bayonet Course.	S.T.P.

S. Philips
Lt.

WAR DIARY or INTELLIGENCE SUMMARY

Army Form C. 2118.

No. 3.

Place	Date 1918	Hour	Summary of Events and Information	Remarks and references to Appendices
ESTAIRES L30.c.	Jan 16		1 Officer & 5 O.R. on leave.	S.S.P.
	17		3 Coys training. 1 Coy employed on work on the Bullet & Bayonet Course.	S.S.P.
			Lieut. If Ifans on leave. 2/Lieut. JD Mackenzie joined the Battalion for duty.	
	18		3 Coys training. 1 Coy employed on work on the Course. 1 NCO to HAVERSKERQUE as Musketry Instructor to Divnl Artillery. 4 O.R. to Course at XV Corps School.	S.S.P.
	19		1 Platoon from 'D' Coy to Brigade School (NEUF BERQUIN). 1 O.R. to First Army School of Cookery BETHUNE. Cpl. B. Richards to UK for Commission.	S.S.P.
	20		Sunday - Services for all denominations. No work on the Course. C.O.'s conference at 5.30pm. 1 NCO to Divisional Signal Camp	S.S.P.
	22		CANDESCURE (F.28 d 30.40). Range allotted to Unit from 2pm. Coys training under Coy Arrangements, also on work, Boxing	S.S.P.

N. T. Sharp

WAR DIARY or INTELLIGENCE SUMMARY N° 4.

Army Form C. 2118.

(Erase heading not required.)

Place	Date	Hour	Summary of Events and Information	Remarks and references to Appendices
	Jan 1918 22			Nil.
	23		Contests held in the evening between the 1st S.W.B. and this Unit. Coys on working parties and Bullet & Bayonet Course, also working under R.E. supervision. Afternoon – Recreational training which included the inter Battalion Cross Country Running Competition 2nd place gained by this Unit.	Nil.
	24		All Coys on work during the morning. Recreational training in the afternoon. Boxing Contest held in the evening between the 16 Welsh Regt and 10th S.W.B. also this Unit.	Nil.
	25		All Coys employed on work under R.E. supervision and also completing the Bullet & Bayonet Course. Recreational training during the afternoon.	Nil.
	26		Coys on work during the morning. Recreational training in the afternoon.	Nil. Lt Phillips

WAR DIARY
or
INTELLIGENCE SUMMARY No. 5

(Erase heading not required.)

Army Form C. 2118.

Place	Date	Hour	Summary of Events and Information	Remarks and references to Appendices
ESTAIRES L.30.c.	1918 Jan 27.		Coys employed on work. Services held for Coys not on work. Inter-Battalion Bombing Competition won by 'B' Coy at the hut.	O.S.
	28.		Coys employed on work. Range allotted to the Battalion. Capt. Z.R. Dale to XV Corps heavy Artillery for insight into the Routine of the Corps heavy C.B. Officers. 2/Lieut. K. Chown on leave.	S.S.
	29.		Coys on work etc. Lecture on Picardo, attended by Officers & Q Runners. 1 NCO to NEUF CHATEL for 10 days Course in horse management.	S.S.
	30.		Coys on work. Baths allotted to "F" head at NEUF BERQUIN. Lecture on Picardo by Col Forgervin.	S.S.
	31.		Coys on working parties during the morning. Lecture at 130 Field Ambulance by Capt. Bliss R.n.T. Baths at NEUF BERQUIN allotted the hut from 9am to 12 noon. Capt A. Seale on leave.	S.S. A.T. Phillips Lt.

P. Welton Captain
Commdg. 17 Bn. R.W. Fus.

WAR DIARY
or
INTELLIGENCE SUMMARY.

Army Form C. 2118.

Ref/ Map 36 N.W.

17 R.W.F.

Place	Date	Hour	Summary of Events and Information	Remarks and references to Appendices
ESTAIRES L 30 C.	1918 Feb. 1.		Working parties supplied for work under R.E. Officer during the morning. Inter-Coy platoon drill Competitions at 2.30 p.m. – won by B Coy. Runners up C Coy. Baths at Nerf Berquin from 9am to 12 noon allotted the unit. Coy at Strength or less.	S.72
	2nd.		Working parties as previous day. All available men on work. During the afternoon the following Inter-Coy Competitions were held – Musketry with Box Respirators on in the alert position – winners C Coy, runners up 'B' Coy. Lewis Gun Competition. Winners B Coy, runners up C coy. 2/Lieut H Chown to XV Corps heavy Artillery for insight for insight into Office routine at C.B. Offices. Range allotted to the unit. The Major General Commanding 38 (Welsh) Division distributed DCM + MM Ribands at 2.30 pm on the Square Estaires. 5517 RSM 13th all. of the unit being the recipient of a DCM riband.	S.72
	3rd		Church Services for all denominations. Baths at Estaires allotted the Battalion from 9am to 12 noon.	S.72
	4th		Working parties under R.E. Officer. All available men from Coys HQ	S.72

26 G
7 sheets

WAR DIARY or INTELLIGENCE SUMMARY

Army Form C. 2118.

Place	Date 1918	Hour	Summary of Events and Information	Remarks and references to Appendices
ESTAIRES L.30.c.	Feb 4th		on work, including Officers. 1 Complete platoon from A coy proceeded to Brigade School near Burguin. Inter-Coy running competition held at 2 pm. Winners "C" Coy, runners up "A" Coy.	S/B
	5th		Working parties supplied in accordance with instructions received. The following NCO's and OR's detailed for duty with the Town Major of Merville & Estaires — Estaires 26 OR's, Merville 3 NCO's & 21 OR's. 8 OR's proceeded to join the 115. T.M. Bty. Also 2/Lieut H.E. Pollicott, 1 groom and 1 clerk sent for duty at Brigade HQ.	S/B
	6th		Working parties supplied as before. 3 OR's joined the Battalion as reinforcements. 1 NCO proceeded on Tunnelling Course. The Baths at Estaires were allotted to Battalion from 8–10am. 2/Lieut J. Williams proceeded to Fletre on advanced course for Battalion Intelligence Officers. The Drums of this Unit, together with the Band of the 10th S.W.B. proceeded by lorries to LESART to play the 2nd Bn. R.W. Fus. to billets at ROBERMETZ.	S/B

WAR DIARY
or
INTELLIGENCE SUMMARY.
(Erase heading not required.)

Army Form C. 2118.

Place	Date	Hour	Summary of Events and Information	Remarks and references to Appendices
ESTAIRES L.30.c.	1918 6/8		6 Officers & 183 O.Rs joined the Battalion as reinforcements from the 15th R.W.F. (2nd: Welch) and posted to Coys.	
	7th		Working parties supplied. The GOC & C.O. inspected the new draft at 2pm. Inter-Coy Cooking Competitions at 4pm. Winners - "B" Coy.	
	8.		Working parties supplied as usual. A Football match was played between the Officers of the 10th S.W.B. and this Unit: result 17 R.W.F. 8 goals - 10 S.W.B. 1 goal. 1 Officer joined joined the Battalion as Reinforcement. 1 NCO from the 13 R.W.F. joined this Unit for one months attachment; being a candidate for Commission.	
	9th		Working Parties supplied as usual. Range allotted to the Battalion. 2/Lieut. W. Hennah & 1 NCO to 2nd Army Centre School of Instruction. The following NCOs of this Unit (attached to 115 Bde HQ & 115 T.M.B. respectively) were awarded the Belgian Croix de Guerre. — 25448 Sergt Owen G. & 25172 Cpl Jones J.	

WAR DIARY
or
INTELLIGENCE SUMMARY

(Erase heading not required.)

Army Form C. 2118.

Place	Date	Hour	Summary of Events and Information	Remarks and references to Appendices
ESTAIRES L.30.c.	10/18	10ᵏ	Sunday. Religious services held for all denominations. Offered S.T. Phillips to XV Corps School for Course in Anti-Aircraft. New Draft proceeded to Working Parties resumed work as on the 9ᵗʰ. All signallers reported to Capt. T.A. Hughes at 3 p.m. Third & fires to Mirvenaux for short Course in "Latest methods of Concealment". Battn. allotted to Battalion from 12 noon to 2 p.m. G. OC Conference at Bac H.Q. 4.30 p.m.	S/B
		11ᵏ	Working Parties supplied as usual. The CO, 2ⁿᵈ in Command, Adjutant and Coy. Officers reconnoitered the new area, leaving Estaires by bus at 5ᵏ. Lieut Col J.B. Cockburn took over Command of the Battalion from Capt P. Brett M.C. 9am. O.R¹ joined the Battalion as reinforcements from the 15ᵗʰ R.W.Fusiliers.	S/B
		12ᵏ	All working parties cancelled. Morning devoted to cleaning up of Billets prior to leaving for the line. Battalion embused at 2.45 pm for Erquinghem and marched from the latter place to WEZ MACQUART area, relieving the 2/5 Kings Own Lancashire Regt. in the line as follows:- Front line - Acoy left, Bcoy right, Subsidiary line, Dcoy left, Ccoy right, BnHQ at I¹⁴.d.4.7.	S/B

WAR DIARY
or
INTELLIGENCE SUMMARY

(Erase heading not required.)

Army Form C. 2118.

Place	Date	Hour	Summary of Events and Information	Remarks and references to Appendices
WEZ MACQUART	Feb 1918 13		(subsidiary line). Transport lines at M 9 a. 9. 8. 2 platoons from Subsidiary line Coys to garrison Jesus Switch. Major P. Welton in Command at the latter place.	—
	14th		Battalion in the line. Capt W Pennington to England on a six months tour.	—
	15th		Battalion in the line. The usual work of maintenance of trenches, wiring & other work carried out by Coys. 1 NCO and 3 ORs to ARMENTIÈRES as town guard.	—
	16.		Battalion in line. 1 OR accidentally wounded whilst cleaning his rifle. 1 OR accidentally killed by a comrade, the latter cleaning his revolver. 1 Officer on leave.	—
	17th		Battalion in the line. Inter-Coy relief, new dispositions of Coys as follows — Front line D Coy left, C Coy right. A Coy left & B Coy right in Subsidiary Line.	—
	18th		Battalion in the line. 1 NCO to UK for Commission. 6 ORs sent to T.M.B. 10 Signallers reported to 116 Bde HQ for Course of instruction. 8 ORs to 115 Bde Pioneer Platoon.	—
	19th		Battalion in the line. 1 NCO to Bethune for interview by R.F.C. Officer. 2 ORs to	—

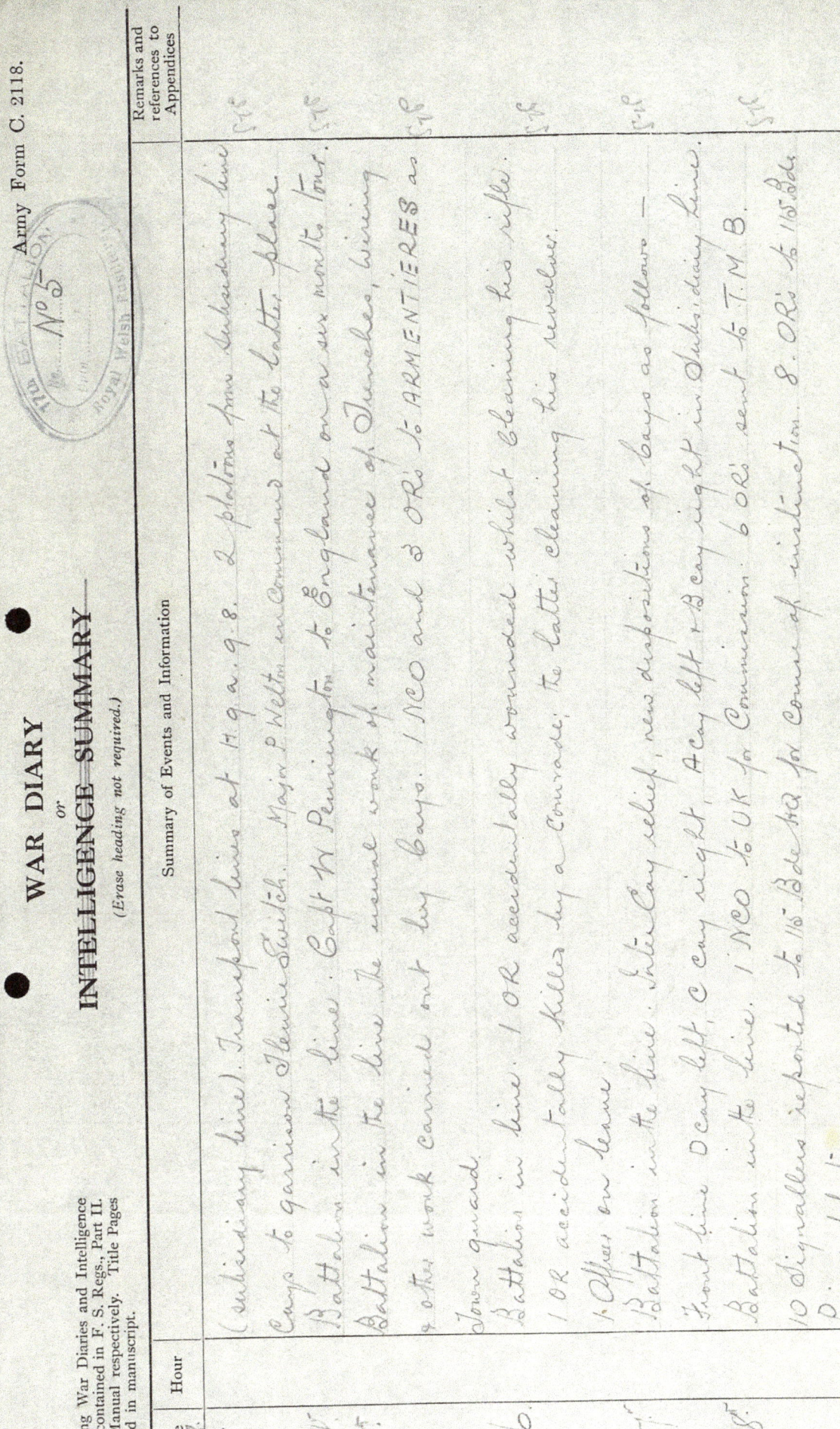

WAR DIARY

INTELLIGENCE SUMMARY

Place	Date 1918	Hour	Summary of Events and Information	Remarks and references to Appendices
WEZ MACQUART.	Jan 19 20.		Divisional Salvage Coy Engineers. Battalion in the line. I.N.C.O. to 1st Tongueset (Lewis Gun Course).	S.S.P S.S.P
	21.		Battalion in the line. 1 NCO + 5 O.Rs to 2 ORs to Merville to Trade Tests. 1 Sergt 1 Cpl + 6 ORs to Bde HQ to relieve guard of 2nd R.W.Fus. Battalion relieved in the line by 2nd R.W.Fus and proceeded to Billets - A, B + C at Rolanderie Farm. D Coy in huts about H.18.C.28 and buildings about H.18.F. Bn HQ at ARTILLERY FARM H.17.d.4.3. Major Welton M.C remained in command at FLEURIE SWITCH. 27 O.Rs joined as reinforcements. 1 OR wounded.	S.S.P
	22nd.		Battalion in reserve line. Batts allotted to the huts from 8 am to 12 noon. 1 NCO on Course.	S.S.P
	23rd -		Battalion in reserve. B Coy on cable burying under Divnl Signal Officer at Farm 45.C.20.20.5. 'D' Coy employed in vicinity of its Billets. 'C' Coy employed E of village of L'ARMEE. A Coy employed S of CROWN PRINCE HOUSE. Court of Enquiry at Bde HQ. Capt. T.A Hughes + 2/Lt Baird attended as members.	S.S.P

WAR DIARY or INTELLIGENCE SUMMARY

Army Form C. 2118.

No. 7.

Place	Date	Hour	Summary of Events and Information	Remarks and references to Appendices
WEZ MACQUART	1918 Feb. 24		Battalion in reserve. Coys employed on work as before. Religious Services for all denominations.	S/R
	25th		1 NCO to UK for Commission. Battalion in reserve. Working parties as before. 2 OR's proceed to Br. as reinforcements. 1 OR to Divn. Farm at Ploegsteert. Board assembles at Bttn. H.Q. attended by M.O. & Senior Line Officer. 1 NCO + XV Corps School on Course.	S/R
	26th		Battalion in reserve. Working parties as before. 1 OR to 22 CCS on Course. Batt attached to B Battalion from 11.30am to 12 noon and 1 pm to 3 pm.	S/R
	27th		Battalion in reserve. Working parties as before. 1 Platoon from 'C' Coy to Brigade School at BLANCHE MAISON A.8.d sheet 36. 2/Lt A Chown to BRUAY to attend a course for Battalion Intelligence Officers.	S/R
	28th		Battalion in reserve. Working parties as usual, every available man on work. G.O.C. Conference at Left Battalion H.Q. at 10 am.	S/R

J.B. Cockburn Lieut Col.
Commanding 17th Bn R.W.F.

WAR DIARY or INTELLIGENCE SUMMARY

Army Form C. 2118.

Place	Date	Hour	Summary of Events and Information	Remarks and references to Appendices
WEZ & MACQUART	1918 March 1st		Coys on work during the morning. Battalion relieved the 2nd R.W.F. in the Wez Macquart sector. Dispositions of Coys as follows – Front line "C" Coy right, "D" Coy left. Subsidiary line "B" Coy right, "A" Coy left. During the march to the line Bde £ (Reserve) were worn.	No. 1.
	2nd		Battalion in the line. A Raiding Party of 3 Officers and 86 O.R.s raided a portion of the enemy's line I.16.d.57.93 to I.16.c.75.05. (Inch TRENCH.) Raiders moved from EVELYN POST to their place of assembly at 11.35 p.m. Zero hour was at 11.50 p.m. The raid was preceded by a well supported artillery bombardment. The result of raid was one prisoner captured. Identifications true. Killed four. Our casualties were thirteen wounded & two subsequently dying from wounds.	£
	3rd		Battalion in the line. Working parties supplied on Trench maintenance and under R.E. supervision.	£
	4th		Battalion in the line. Working parties supplied as previous day.	£

WAR DIARY
or
INTELLIGENCE SUMMARY.
(Erase heading not required.)

Army Form C. 2118.

No 2.

Place	Date	Hour	Summary of Events and Information	Remarks and references to Appendices
WEZ MACQUART.	1918 March 5th		Battalion in the line. Working parties supplied.	
	6th		Battalion in the line. Working parties supplied.	
	7th		Battalion in the line. Working parties supplied.	
	8th		Battalion in the line. A Lg of War party took place between "C" Coy and a company of the 14th R.W.F. "D" Company were the winners. The above competition was the semi-final of Divisional Competition.	
	9th		Battalion in the line. Battalion relieved by the 2nd R.W.F and proceeded to billets in ROLANDERIE FARM. Batt. HQ. at ARTILLERY FARM.	
	10th		No work for coys. Battalion HQ. vacated ARTILLERY FARM. owing to hostile shelling and established themselves at ROLANDERIE FARM. Instruction received for 33% of battalion including specialists to proceed to STEENWERCH immediately. Full Lewis also sent. Major Welch M.C. O.C. Details. Battalion in reserve. All available men on working parties reporting to R.E. Officer at A.17.d.4.8. Billets allotted the Battalion at JESUS FARM.	
	11th			

Army Form C. 2118.

No 3.

WAR DIARY
or
INTELLIGENCE SUMMARY.
(Erase heading not required.)

Instructions regarding War Diaries and Intelligence Summaries are contained in F. S. Regs., Part II. and the Staff Manual respectively. Title pages will be prepared in manuscript.

Place	Date	Hour	Summary of Events and Information	Remarks and references to Appendices
WEZ MACQUART	1918 March 12th		Battalion in reserve. Working parties as previous day.	
	13th		Battalion in reserve. Working parties for half day only. Night carrying party of 366 O.R. supplied for Special Coy R.E.	
	14th		Battalion in reserve. No work for men employed on carrying party previous night. Night carrying party of 1 & 7 O.R.'s for Special Coy R.E.	
	15th		Battalion on Working Parties.	
	16th		Battalion in reserve. Guard supplied for Brigade HQ. All available men on work & tools washing centre allotted to the Battalion from 1pm to 5pm.	
	17th		Battalion relieved the 2nd R.W.F. in the Wez Macquart Sector. dispositions :- Right "D" Coy. Reg. Centre "A" Coy. Reg. Centre "B" Coy. Left "C" Coy.	
	18th		Battalion in the line. Sergeant Owen 25781 and Private E. Bryford O.C.M. 33307 awarded M.M. for gallantry and devotion to duty during raid on enemy trenches on Night 23 March.	

WAR DIARY
INTELLIGENCE SUMMARY

Army Form C. 2118.

No 4.

Place	Date	Hour	Summary of Events and Information	Remarks and references to Appendices
W F 2 MACQUART	1918 March 18th		L/Cpl W Mulvey 55634 awarded Meritorious Service Certificate for good work during the raid. Casualties 1 OR. wounded. 8 OR. gassed	
	19th		Battalion in the line. 2 Officers & 5th OR's proceeded to Brigade School. Casualties 3 OR. wounded. At 11 pm a howitzer gas Bombardment was projected into and near Maquart village. Casualties 1 OR. wounded.	
	20th		Battalion in the line. Casualties 1 OR. wounded	
	21st		Battalion in the line.	
	22nd			
	23rd			
	24th			
	25th		Draft of 8 ORs arrived. Battalion relieved by 2/nd R.W.F. then proceeded to billets in Pelandrie Farm.	
	26th		In the 13th R.W.F. on the left subsector of the Wez Macquart Sector. Battalion relieved the 13th R.W.F. on the left subsector. Dispositions. "A" Coy front line. "D" Coy Subsidiary line. "C" Coy in support. "B" Coy of Annie switch.	
	27th		Battalion in the line. At 3.45 am the battalion on our right	
	28th			

Army Form C. 2118.

No 5.

WAR DIARY
or
INTELLIGENCE SUMMARY.

(Erase heading not required.)

1/7 BATTALION
Royal Welsh Fusiliers

Place	Date	Hour	Summary of Events and Information	Remarks and references to Appendices
WE Z MACQUART.	28th (cont)		Plant made a raid on enemy trenches. In retaliation enemy heavily shelled our sector. Casualties 2 killed 3 wounded	
	29th		Battalion in the line. Casualties 1 killed & wounded Battalion relieved in the line by the 2/4th Royal North Lancs Regt. Bn proceeded to billets at Mouveaux Monde arriving at 1 am. 30th	
	30th		Battalion proceeded to Sauchberque arriving at 4 pm	
	31st		Battalion told in divers-bergue. Training carried on under Coy arrangements. Special attention being paid to musketry	

A Read
Capt
Adjutant
Commanding 1/7 Bn R.W.F.

115th Inf.Bde.
38th Div.

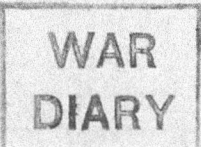

17th BATTN. THE ROYAL WELCH FUSILIERS.

A P R I L

1 9 1 8

WAR DIARY

INTELLIGENCE SUMMARY

17 R W F   Army Form C. 2118.

Vol 29 No 1

Place	Date	Hour	Summary of Events and Information	Remarks and references to Appendices
	1918	Map Ref. sheet 57 D S.E.		
	April 1st		Battalion left HAVERSKERQUE at 8 a.m. and marched to CROIX-S-WS. station arriving at the latter place about 10.30 a.m. Train departed at noon, "A" Company entrained at HAVERSKERQUE and entrained at 9 p.m. Battalion arrived at DOULLENS Stn. at 6 p.m. and marched to VILLERS BOCAGE arriving in billets by 11.30 p.m. During the march from HAVERSKERQUE to CROIX-WS, Pt. Marks. 10,000 of "A" Co. and nurse Muncy on the canal and was in imminent danger of drowning but for the timely assistance of 2/Lt. J.O. Mackenzie who dived into the canal and rescued him.	K
Hedauville V.3.v.c.x.9	April 2nd		Battalion moved from VILLIERS BOCAGE at 11.15 a.m. and marched to HEDAUVILLE via WARLOY arriving in billets at 7-8 p.m. All companys billeted in the village. Captain A.H. Leed in command of the Battalion	K
	3rd		Colonel Roberts assumed Command of Brigade. Boy Commanders and N.C.O.s reconnoitred the line. 175 ORs on working parties.	K
	4th		Battalion at HEDAUVILLE. Men on working parties previous night. Roads carried out under Coy arrangements. Reeling in its morning.	K
	5th		Battalion at HEDAUVILLE. Parade under Coy arrangements. Pang C.S.M. Clarke A.G.S. of Battalion also disposal of kit for inspection of PT + B.F. A working party of 150 ORs + 350 ORs found 1st 21/2 Bn for Reinforcements. near ENGLEBELMER.	K

28 G 4 sheets

WAR DIARY
INTELLIGENCE SUMMARY

Army Form C. 2118.

N₀ 2

Place	Date	Hour	Summary of Events and Information	Remarks and references to Appendices
HEDAUVILLE V.34.c.4.9	April 1918 6th		Battalion at HEDAUVILLE. Parades carried out under Coy arrangements. Range allotted to 2 Coys. 10 PR forced the battalion to keep furnaces alight. M.O. referred from leave and assumed command of the Batn.	
	7th		Religious services for all denominations held in the morning. Operation orders received. Working party S.O.S. 350 PR. Branches to work under C.R.E. at 12 noon. Battalion moved from HEDAUVILLE at 6-5 pm and marched to HERRISSART. Battalion to billets arriving at about 11 pm.	
	8th		Battalion at HERRISSART. Working party of 600 OR for work under C.R.E. at 2 pm. Cokers reconnoitred the Inde.	
	9th		Battalion at HERRISSART. Parades under Coy arrangements. Ratio of TOUTENCOURT allotted to Battalion for reinforcements.	
	10th		Battalion at HERRISSART. Parades carried on under Coy arrangements.	
	11th		Battalion at HERRISSART. Parades carried out under Coy arrangements. At 9 pm. Battalion marched to HENENCOURT via CONTAY. Arrived in billets at Battle surplus remained at CONTAY.	
	12th		HENENCOURT at about 10 pm. Casualties 4 O.R.s wounded. Battalion moved from HENENCOURT at 9 pm and bivouaced on ridge immediately S.E. of SENLIS.	
	13th		Battalion spent the day improving bivouacs. Casualties 2 O.R. killed & 6 O.R. wounded.	

Army Form C. 2118.

No 3

WAR DIARY
or
INTELLIGENCE SUMMARY.
(Erase heading not required.)

Place	Date	Hour	Summary of Events and Information	Remarks and references to Appendices
SENLIS V.16.b.8.8	April 1916 14th		Battalion spent the day improving bivouac.	
	15th		Parades under Coy arrangements. Particular attention being paid to musketry. Colonel Lockhart received command of the Battalion.	
	16th		Parades under Coy arrangements. Particular attention being paid to musketry. Working parties supplied during the night for track digging in the old trench lines. 10 O.R. of first battalion wounded.	
	17th		Battalion on working party during the night for trench digging in the old trench lines. Other period of battalion as reinforcement.	
	18th		Battalion relieved the 1st R.W.F. in the Bouzincourt Sector. Dugudration's Regt. "A" Coy. Centre. "B" Coy Regt to "C" coy. Support "D" Coy. 1 O.R. accidentally wounded.	
BOUZINCOURT W13 a 9.9	19th		Battalion in the line. Casualties 2 O.R. wounded.	
	20th		Battalion in the line. Casualties 1 O.R. killed 1 Off & 4 O.R's wounded.	
	21st		Battalion relieved in the BOUZIN COURT Sector by portions of the 13th, 14th & 16th R.W.F. who took up attack positions. Battalion proceeded to bivouacs on the N.W. slope of ridge immediately S.E. of SENLIS. Casualties 2 O.R killed & 3 O.R's wounded. 1 Off and 34 OR's joined the battalion as reinforcements.	

WAR DIARY or INTELLIGENCE SUMMARY

Army Form C. 2118.

No 4

Place	Date	Hour	Summary of Events and Information	Remarks and references to Appendices
SENLIS V.16.b.&.c.	April 1918 2nd		Battn in bivouac. Battn allotted to fatigue battalion all day. 1 off. & 1 O.R. joined the battalion as reinforcements.	
	23rd		Battn in bivouac. Battn allotted to fatigue battalion all day. Working parties of 3 coys. found digging & 1 coy moving in the line. 9 O.R's joined the battalion as reinforcements during the night.	
	24th		Battalion in reserve. One company detailed for digging in the line during the night. Casualties 1 O.R. killed 10 O.R. wounded.	
BOUZINCOURT W.13.a.9.9	25th		Battalion relieved the 13th & 16th R.I.R. & 5 Y. & L. Reg. in the BOUZINCOURT SECTOR. Dispositions Right "A" Coy Centre "B" Coy Left "C" Coy Reserve "D" Coy in Bouzincourt Support.	
	26th		Battalion in the line. Casualties 2 O.R's killed & 10 O.R's wounded.	
	27th		Battalion in the line. Casualties 2 O.R's killed & 3 O.R's wounded.	
	28th		Battalion in the line. Casualties 1 off. wounded 1 O.R. killed & 2 O.R's wounded.	
	29th		Battalion in the line.	
	30th		Battalion in the line. 1 off. joined battalion as reinforcement.	

J.B. Cockburn Bt/Col
Commanding 1/8th R.D. Fus.

Army Form C. 2118.

WAR DIARY
or
INTELLIGENCE SUMMARY.
(Erase heading not required.)

17th Batt'n Royal Welsh Fus'rs

Vol 30

Place	Date	Hour	Summary of Events and Information	Remarks and references to Appendices
Bouzincourt	1918 May 1st		Battalion in the line. At 12.30 am under a barrage of Stokes Mortars two platoons of "D" Coy under the command of Capt. J.C. Gledhill made an attack on the enemy's post in the vicinity of Love Tree W.15.b.0.5. The objective was not reached owing to enemy heavy Machine Gun fire, but the men advanced 20 yards on the left and about 100 yds on the right and consolidated position thus forming an extension of the enemy trench in the valley below. 1 officer wounded (2/Lt) 8 O.R. killed 21 O.R wounded 1 O.R. missing.	
	2nd		Battalion in the line. B. Relieved by the 2nd R.W.F. and proceeded to bivouac on the N.W. slope of ridge immediately S.E of Senlis. 11 hrs found the Battalion so far required. Casualties Nil.	
X.16.c.8.8.	3rd		Bn in reserve. During the night 3 Coys supplied for working party digging trenches in Corps Line. Casualties Nil.	
	4th		Bn in reserve. Working party supplied during the night for trench digging in Corps Line. 1 Officer joined the Battalion as reinforcement.	
	5th		Bn in reserve. Total working parties during the night 2 Officers and 120 OR.	
	6th		B in reserve. Battalion so far required.	
	7th		Bn in reserve. Normal working parties during the night.	
	8th		Bn in reserve. Moved during the afternoon & 2 in coys 2 R.W. & 1 in coy 29 Dublin to S.E. of Bouzincourt sector. Support A Coy - Reserve D Coy - Brigaders left B Coy 150 O.R. joined the Battalion as reinforcements	29 R Dublin

WAR DIARY
INTELLIGENCE SUMMARY

Army Form C. 2118.

No 2

Place	Date 1915 May	Hour	Summary of Events and Information	Remarks and references to Appendices
BOEZINGHE	9th		Battalion in the line. 1 Officer killed. 2 ORs killed.	AG
	10th		" " " Officer joined the battalion as reinforcement. Casualties	AG
	11th		2 Officers wounded. 7 Dawn 2527 awarded M.M. for gallantry when on duty whilst in charge of transport when under heavy shell fire.	AG
	12th		2 ORs wounded 2 ORs killed	AG
	13th		Bn in the line. Casualties 3 ORs wounded	AG
	14th		" " 3 ORs killed 12 ORs joined the battalion as reinforcements	AG
	15th		Bn in the line. Casualties 6 ORs wounded	AG
	16th		" " " 1 OR killed	
	17th		" "	AG
	18th		" "	
	19th		" Casualties 5 ORs killed 6 ORs wounded	AG
	20th		Bn relieved by the 15th Cheshires, was proceeded to march to Henneuil. During relief BOEZINCOURT was bombarded from 10h to 11.30am and for little shell intervals near HOOGEMEELE for continued march to MR JOHR via crossing here at 9.30am. The remainder of the day was devoted to cleaning up. Battalion allotted to the Brigadier M. Genl Pictures & all Officers by the Corps Commanding officers. As a result of heavy gun bombardment during relief 1 Officer was found.	AG
	21st		LtGen MGC Riseto QR5360 awarded the DCM and Corpl W Rafford wounded the MM for gallantry & attention to duty during attack on enemy trenches on the 14th May	AG

Army Form C. 2118.

No 3

WAR DIARY
INTELLIGENCE SUMMARY.
(Erase heading not required.)

Place	Date	Hour	Summary of Events and Information	Remarks and references to Appendices
HERSART	23rd April 1917		Training as per Brigade Training Scheme. Including musketry close order drill and recreational training.	
	24th		Companies fired their first Brigade Class. The MG range at T.22 central. The officers and the Coy arrangements including musketry etc. Training carried out under Coy arrangements including musketry etc. During the afternoon the Battalion attended the inspection of the Brigade by the Brigade General.	
	25th		Church Parade for all denominations during the day. Kit inspection of the Battalion carried out by the Commanding Officer. 50 O.R's joined the Battalion as reinforcements.	
	26th		Coy arrangements for musketry etc. During the afternoon the Battalion attended a Brigade Parade for the Corps Commander's inspection. The Corps Commander presented Military Medals to Cpl. T. Davis & Corpl D. Pickford.	
	27th		In conjunction with the 2nd R.D.F. the Battalion took part in a tactical exercise with tanks. Musketry recreational training carried out during the afternoon under Coy arrangements.	
	28th		B.M. visited the battalion all day. Men passed through the Gas Chamber. Recreational training, musketry etc. carried out under Coy arrangements. In the evening a concert was held by the Battalion.	
	29th			

Army Form C. 2118.

WAR DIARY
~~INTELLIGENCE SUMMARY.~~
(Erase heading not required.)

Instructions regarding War Diaries and Intelligence Summaries are contained in F. S. Regs., Part II. and the Staff Manual respectively. Title pages will be prepared in manuscript.

Place	Date	Hour	Summary of Events and Information	Remarks and references to Appendices
MERISART	29th 30th		Battalion Bayonet Competition held. Won by H Coy. Recreational training, musketry &c carried out under Coy arrangements	
	31st		Brigade Tactical Scheme carried out by skeleton HQ's and Platoon officers. Rest for batches nods of arrangements	

P. Welton Major
Commanding 17th Bn. R.B. L

WAR DIARY
or
INTELLIGENCE SUMMARY.

Army Form C. 2118.

17 RWF
Vol 31

Place	Date	Hour	Summary of Events and Information	Remarks and references to Appendices
HERRISART	JUNE 1918	—	Brigade Competition held during the day.	
			Coy Competition. Musketry. 17th R.W.F. 2nd	
			Lewis Gun do do 3rd	
			P.Y. do do 2nd	
			Bomb do do 2nd	
			Lewis do do 1st	
			Signalling do do 2nd	
			Stokes Mortar do do 1st	
			Bullet & Bayonet do Tactical Scheme do 3rd	
			Run do do Steadiness of Sentries do 1st	
			Flag & Star (O.R.) do do 1st	
			do do (Officers) do do 1st	
			100 yds Race do do 2nd	
			Long Jump do do 1st	
			High do do do 2nd	
			A.R.A. Competition do do 2nd	
			Bruch. Services held during the day. Divisional Competitions held.	
HERRISART	2nd	—	A.R.A. Competition 17th R.W.F. 2nd	
			Rapid firing do Musketry do 1st	
			Snap Shooting do do 1st	
HERRISART	3rd	—	Brigadier presented Silver Bugle to "D" Company in the evening. Parades under Company arrangements for Musketry etc.	

WAR DIARY
or
INTELLIGENCE SUMMARY.
(Erase heading not required.)

Army Form C. 2118.

Place	Date	Hour	Summary of Events and Information	Remarks and references to Appendices
HERRISART	4th	–	Battalion left Herrisart at 9 a.m. and marched to Bivouac in Divisional Reserve. MESNIL SECTOR arriving at 1.30 p.m. and a relief reported complete at 2.55 p.m. Unit relieved BRAKE Bn. 63rd Division.	
Divisional Reserve	5th	–	Training under Company arrangements. Musketry, Lewis Gun, "B" Coy.	
do.	6th	–	1 Officer & 2 NCOs per Company reconnoitred forward positions. Training continued under Company arrangements in the morning and afternoon and at 11 pm relieved the 11th WELSH Regt. in SUPPORT and the right of ENGLE-BELMER. Relief reported complete at 2 am. (7th June.)	
Support RIGHT ENGLE-BELMER	7th	–	Officers & NCOs reconnoitred forward positions. Work done in improving Bivouacs & Shelters, also digging lines. Enemy casualties 1 OR wounded at duty.	
do.	8th	–	Work in improving dools and Battle positions also shelters. In the night of the 8th/9th our Artillery put up a barrage on enemy lines while the troops on our left carried out a raid at HAMEL. Casualties 6 OR wounded.	
do.	9th	–	The same work as on previous day was carried on. Officers & NCOs from each Company reconnoitred forward positions. In the evening transport bringing supplies shelled near Bn. Hdqrs. One horse killed & 1 horse wounded. 1 OR to Lewis Gun Course at LEAVILLERS. 6 OR. to T.M Course at LEAVILLERS.	

Place	Date	Hour	Summary of Events and Information	Remarks and references to Appendices
SUPPORT. RIGHT. ENGLE-BELMER	10th	-	C.O. & Adjutant reconnoitered front line. One Officer & one N.C.O. per Coy. went to take over new positions in relieving 10th S.W.B. 13th done, improving Shelters by day and rally done by night. 10th, 11th and relief reported complete at 1.55 a.m. (11th June) Casualties 1 O.R.	E.E.Lloyd H.
FRONT LINE.	11th	-	13th done improving Coys. & lines. Enemy attacked one of our posts but was repulsed leaving one dead man firm. Identification was secured. 15th took over another Company front relieving # a Company of the 2nd Batt. R.W.F. on our left. Relief complete at 10 p.m. Casualties 2 O.R.	E.E.Lloyd H.
do.	12th	-	Batt. relieved by 13th WELSH Regt. Relief complete at 1-30 a.m. arrived at Divisional Reserve Area at 4 a.m. 13th.	E.E.Lloyd H.
Divisional Reserve Area PUCHEVILLERS	13th	-	Batt. rested during the morning - cleaning & making up of equipment during afternoon. Baths in the evening.	E.E.Lloyd H.
do.	14th	-	C. Coy placed under orders of 2nd R.W.F. for 14th & 15th A+B working parties. D Coy having Baths all day.	E.E.Lloyd H.
do.	15th	-	A.B & D Coys working parties and carrying Experimental Trench Mortar exploded in near vicinity of camp at 7.30am. Baths in the	E.E.Lloyd H.

Army Form C. 2118.

WAR DIARY
or
INTELLIGENCE SUMMARY.
(Erase heading not required.)

Instructions regarding War Diaries and Intelligence Summaries are contained in F. S. Regs., Part II. and the Staff Manual respectively. Title pages will be prepared in manuscript.

Place	Date	Hour	Summary of Events and Information	Remarks and references to Appendices
Divisional Horse Area. FORCEVILLE	15th	-	14 OR. proceeded to Lewis Gun Course B/S. 6 OR. do on T.M. course at LEAVILLERS.	Lt. Lloyd
do	16th	-	A B & C Companies working parties Chuck Burroo morning & evening. One Officer per day & HQ reconnoitred a gun position P25a. 25.4.5.	Lt. Lloyd
do	17th	-	All Companies working & carrying. One Officer & 6 OR attend F.G.C.M. of Pte. J.M. Jones & Pte. 15. Burrows at LEAVILLERS.	Lt. Lloyd
do	18th	-	All Companies working & carrying parties. 5 Officers & 8 Gunners reconnoitred new line. 1 camp shelled by H.V. gun casualties 1 OR killed & 4 OR wounded.	Lt. Lloyd
do	19th	-	All Companies working & carrying parties. Five Officers reconnoitring new position. Batn. HQ moved to Billet 52 in FORCEVILLE. Draft of 46 arrived to Batn. casualties 2 OR wounded.	Lt. Lloyd
do	20th	=	All Companies working & carrying parties. Three NCOs to Corps School. Two Officers reconnoitred new position.	Lt. Lloyd
do	21st	-	C.O. & Adjutant reconnoitred new position. also 5 Officers & NCOs carrying & working parties as usual	Lt. Lloyd

WAR DIARY
or
INTELLIGENCE SUMMARY

Army Form C. 2118.

Place	Date	Hour	Summary of Events and Information	Remarks and references to Appendices
Divisional Reserve Area FORCEVILLE.	22nd	—	All Companies working & carrying parties. Batt relieved 16th Batt. R.W.F. in MESNIL-LEFT SECTOR A,C,& D Coys in the line. B Coy in Support. Batt HdQrs Q.28.a.9.8. Relief completed at 12.45 am. Casualties. 2/Lt G.E. Howell 10R killed & 8 O.R. wounded.	E.E. Lloyd M/-
MESNIL LEFT SECTOR	23rd	—	Battalion in the line. Casualties Nil	E.E. Lloyd M/- E.E. Lloyd M/-
do	24th	—	Battalion in the line. Casualties Nil	E.E. Lloyd M/-
do	25th	—	Battalion in the line. Major H.V. Evans relieved Major G. Bellew in the line. 1/Batt R.W.F. carried out a Minor Operation on suspected enemy posts. Posts were not occupied. Two O.R. went to T.M. Bomb Casualties	E.E. Lloyd M/- E.E. Lloyd M/-
do	26th	—	Battalion in the line. Two O.R. wounded	E.E. Lloyd M/- E.E. Lloyd M/-
do	27th	—	Batt in the line. Batt relieved by 10th K.S.W.Bs. On relief all Companies proceeded to PURPLE LINE. Batt HdQrs at Q.19.a.9.1. Relief completed 12.55 am. Casualties. 1 O.R. wounded. Two Officers proceeded on a Course. Batt relieved 1/Batt. HdQrs Q.2/a.1.9.	E.E. Lloyd M/-
do	28th	—	RIGHT SUPPORT Coys on Intercompany bzggln along Durional Road. Relief completed 1.40 am. * 1/4th Batt WELSH REGT + 1/4th Batt. /RWF+	E.E. Lloyd M/-

WAR DIARY
or
INTELLIGENCE SUMMARY.
(Erase heading not required.)

Army Form C. 2118.

Place	Date	Hour	Summary of Events and Information	Remarks and references to Appendices
Lote military system RIGHT	29th	—	Batt. in Intermediary System. 16 men proceeded to TOUTENCOURT to be inspected by Inspector of crafts. Casualties 10R killed 7 OR wounded.	E.E./Hyde/ff
do.	30th	—	Batt. in Intermediary System. In conjunction on fours Gun Course 58 Division on our right front a Minor Operation which proved successful.	E.E./Hyde/ff

LtC Vincent Evans

Major

Commdg 14 Bn M.E.R.

H.Q 115" Infy Bde.   Ref. Y.

Herewith War Diary of this
Unit for the month of July 1918

                                    Sgd Davis
2/8/18   Lieut & A/Adjt
                                    17 Rct

WAR DIARY
INTELLIGENCE SUMMARY

17th Batt Royal Welch Fusiliers

Army Form C. 2118.

Place	Date	Hour	Summary of Events and Information	Remarks and references to Appendices
Wednesday System 1	July 1st		Battalion in Intervening of time. Bn relieved by 16th R.W.F. and proceeded to FORCEVILLE. Reserve area.	
	2nd		3 spare day to cleaning up and resting	
	3rd		3 Resting and working parties 36 O.R's.	
	4th		B. Resting & in trenches. L.G. firing & practise trench Billets allotted to 6 B. from 8 am — 12.30 pm	
	5		B. working Rt Col & Lt Norman DSO took command of the battalion	
	6th		Two Coys training 2 Coys working two Off's wounded 1st Batt Glow & 38 O.R. joined the battalion as reinforcements from 7.30 am C & D Coys on range for PZII C.3 ×	
	7th		On marching and resting	
	8th		B. working and cooking Officers rejoined returned Rifle line	
MESNIL LEFT SECTION	9th		B. relieved 1/R. Welch P.O.5 in the line on left of Ancry Wood Subsection A Coy Left B. Coy Right D. Coy in support. C Coy attached to 13th R.W.J. Relief Complete at 1 am.	

WAR DIARY
INTELLIGENCE SUMMARY.
(Erase heading not required.)

Army Form C. 2118.

Place	Date	Hour	Summary of Events and Information	Remarks and references to Appendices
MESNIL LEFT SECTOR	July 11th		Got outfit ready for enemy trenches for information purposes	
	12th		2nd R.W.F. raided HAMEL. Making this part an our left front. They collected 1 M.G. & 18 prisoners	
			Got our ruthram at 1am. 10.2.15.a.m. for our operator	
			Got our ruthram attack in HAMEL. Working party of 100 men supplied for cable burying. Casualties 8 but wounded.	
	13th		At 1 a.m. 1 officer & 20 o.r. raided an enemy post in the valley leading party entered the post after cutting through much wire. Post was found empty but found again fit occupation. 2/Lt Riccio and 2 o.r. supply party of 100 men cable burying. Casualties 1 officer & 8 o.rs. wounded.	
			Laying reinforcements	
	14th		1 Officer & 6 o.r. Raiders recounted line. Working party of 100 men supplied for burying cable. Casualties 1 o.r. wounded. Working party on Cable Burying	
	15th		Casualties 3 o.r. wounded. Casualties 1 o.r. wounded	
	16th		Bn. in line. Working party cable burying. Recall of Wycheatups gas attack	

Army Form C. 2118.

No 3

WAR DIARY
or
INTELLIGENCE SUMMARY.

(Erase heading not required.)

Instructions regarding War Diaries and Intelligence Summaries are contained in F. S. Regs., Part II. and the Staff Manual respectively. Title pages will be prepared in manuscript.

Place	Date 1918	Hour	Summary of Events and Information	Remarks and references to Appendices
MESNIL LEFT SECTOR	July 17th		Battalion in the line. Officers & 7 O.R. reported from Casualties	
"	18th		Relieved by the 7th Royal Fusiliers. Relief complete 2am 19th. Casualties 1 O.R. wounded. 1 O.R. joined bn. as reinforcement.	
HERRISART	19th		Bn. marched to Senlincourt arriving at 10.30am having halted at Senlincourt at 8am for three hours.	
	20th		Remainder of the day spent in cleaning up. Day devoted to cleaning up and an inspection by the Commanding Officer. 214114 R.Q.M.S. Bone L.S. awarded the Meritorious Service Medal	
	21st		"B" Coy. musketry on range. The remaining coys. carried out training as directed by the Commanding Officer.	
	22nd		"E" Coy. musketry on range. Remaining coys. carried out training as directed by the C.O. Both allotted to the L/S. Sergt. throughout the day. 13573 Pte. J. Hopwood awarded the Military Medal for gallantry and devotion to duty.	
	23rd		"H" & "B" Coys. musketry on range. Remaining coys. on parade throughout the day and coy. arrangements. 1 Subaltern & 27 O.R. joined the Bn. as reinforcements.	

WAR DIARY
INTELLIGENCE SUMMARY

Army Form C. 2118.

Place	Date 1916	Hour	Summary of Events and Information	Remarks and references to Appendices
HERRISART	July 24th		B Coy on B.B. course (T.9.b). The remaining Coys training as directed by the Commanding Officer. During the afternoon the Divisional Band played in the Chateau.	
	25th		D Coy musketry on range. Remaining Coys training as directed by the Commanding Officer.	
	26th		1 Officer & 32 O.Rs joined the Battalion as reinforcements. A Coy musketry on range. Remaining Coys training in Coys.	
	27th		C.O. & O.C. Coys reconnoitred Brown Road. Training as directed by the Commanding Officer. All also saw box Respirators.	
	28th		E Coy on musketry range. Remainder of the Coys training as directed by the C.O.	
	29th		T.6. T.6.T.6 & T.6. to be Lieutenants known Killed during the day. Two wounded. In the information received for infection by the Commanding Officer. Brigade Sports field on the afternoon 1&5 feet no arrangements at B.HQ at pg 3 2 4	
ACHEUX	30th		B.work from Herrisart to Acheux Coys — pg 4 C of 1	
	31st		At 9 am Coy C.O. of New Battalion ran. Duly the day A&B Coys signalled together. the Commanding Officer C&D Coys platoon training.	

O'Connor Lt Col
Commanding 1st R.D.F.

17 RWF
1/5
Vol 33
32B
H5766

WAR DIARY
or
INTELLIGENCE SUMMARY.

(Erase heading not required.)

Army Form C. 2118.

Place	Date	Hour	Summary of Events and Information	Remarks and references to Appendices
FCHEUX	1918 Aug 1st		Coys carried out training, including Musketry & open warfare as detailed by the Commanding Officer	
"	2		do	
"	3		do	
"	4		do	
BOUZINCOURT	5		Battalion relieved the 7 Bn. East Yorks in support in the BOUZINCOURT SECTOR	
"	6		Battalion in support in the BOUZINCOURT SECTOR Casualties Nil.	
"			"	4 OR Killed
"			"	1 OR "

P. Welton Major
Commdg. 17th R.W. Fus.

WAR DIARY
or
INTELLIGENCE SUMMARY

Army Form C. 2118.

Place	Date	Hour	Summary of Events and Information	Remarks and references to Appendices
BOUZINCOURT	10		Battalion in support in the BOUZINCOURT SECTOR	
	11		Battalion relieved the 2nd Bn. R.W.F in the front line.	
	12		Dispositions D Coy left, C Coy right front, B Coy left support, A Coy right support	
	13		do	
	14		do	
	15		do	
	16		do	
	17		do	
	18		Advance party of 3/318 American Infy Regt arrived to take over but all orders were cancelled. Battalion in line.	
	19		do. Inter Company Relief. B Coy left front, A Coy Right front, C Coy Right Support, D Coy Left Support	
	20		do	
	21		do	
	22		do	

P. Welson Major
Commanding 17th Bn R.W. Fus.

Army Form C. 2118.

WAR DIARY
or
INTELLIGENCE SUMMARY.
(Erase heading not required.)

Instructions regarding War Diaries and Intelligence Summaries are contained in F. S. Regs., Part II. and the Staff Manual respectively. Title pages will be prepared in manuscript.

Place	Date 1916	Hour	Summary of Events and Information	Remarks and references to Appendices
BOUZINCOURT	Aug 23rd		Battalion moved to the Eastern side of the river Ancre and relieved the 13th R.W.F.	
	24th		At 1 a.m. under a heavy artillery barrage, the Battalion in conjunction with the 2nd R.W.F. on the left and the 113th Brigade on the right attacked the enemy line. The Battalion attacked on a frontage of about 500 yards with "B" Coy. left front. "A" right front and "C" & "D" in support. The Battalion advanced about 1000 yds and was then held up by heavy M.G. fire. The Battalion captured 200 prisoners and a number of M.G.'s. "A" & "B" Coys advanced into a post of M Guns and were almost surrounded but fought their way through. Casualties 6 officers and about 100 O.R's. About 6 p.m. troops assembled, at Crucifix Corner and marched across country by compass bearing to a mile N.W. of Pozières.	
	25th		Battalion rested 2 hours in trenches. At 3 a.m. marched by compass bearing to 1000 yds N.W. of Mametz Wood, where Battalion bivouaced for the day and night whilst 2 R.W.F. and 10th S.W.B. got into touch with the enemy in Mametz Wood and North of Mametz Wood respectively.	
	26th		At 10 a.m. Battalion advanced in artillery formation across country and took High Wood, capturing 1 M Gun and 5 prisoners. Battalion held the line N.E. and E. of High Wood. Enemy holding ground further East strongly with M Guns and snipers.	
	27th		114th Brigade passed through 115 Brigade and attacked under a barrage, advancing 1200 yards whilst the shell fire consolidated. 115 (Bde. advancing) held ground up to northern Hag yds B.1146 R.16.	

P. Welsey Wynn
17 K.R.W.F
[signature] 7/13 R.B.

WAR DIARY
or
INTELLIGENCE SUMMARY.

(Erase heading not required.)

Army Form C. 2118.

Place	Date	Hour	Summary of Events and Information	Remarks and references to Appendices
Field	1918 Aug 29	5 AM	At 5 AM Bourbon under cover of barrage attacked the enemy & having relieved the 11th Bde., the latter clearing Delville Wood on the Right Flank. Order of attack – 11B Regt. 10. S.W.B. Left front. 17th R.W.F. Right front. 2nd R.W.F. support. The enemy encountered up to 3000 yds. & counted enemy on ground 1500yds W. of Morval which was strongly held by M. Guns Casualties not yet ascertained.	
	30	10th	10th S.W.B's advanced and captured Les Boeufs & been held up by M. Gun fire. 2nd R.W.F has been moved up in support to 1/2 pre B behind Les Boeufs.	
	31		Battalion rested the day.	

P. Welton Maj.
Commdg 17th R.W.F.

WAR DIARY
or
INTELLIGENCE SUMMARY.
(Erase heading not required.)

Army Form C. 2118.

17 RWF 115/38

Place	Date	Hour	Summary of Events and Information	Remarks and references to Appendices
	Sept. 1st	4H.45am	The 114th Bde. attacked and captured the village of MORVAL. At 5.10 A.M. the 115th Inf. Bde. R.W.F. Lt.Fs + 10th S.W.B. in Support. Attack proceeded on front of 115th RWF right, 2nd R.W.F. Lt.Fs + 10th S.W.B. in Support. Attack proceeded at first up to within 1500 yds but attack by 17th Dragoon on the left. The 17th Dragoon on the right did not come up. French the 17th Bn. was enfiladed by the enemy and forced to retire. The 300 yds in front of MORVAL Division in large numbers were captured by the Bn. also light batten MGs.	
MORVAL		6pm	The Battalion was re-organised ready for further operations. A result of successful attack from a SW direction on SAILLY-SAILLISEL by 113th Division as a natural result of MORVAL	EEB
do.	2nd		and 115th Inf. Bde. 17th RWF in Support. On nature at 5pm being position EAST of SAILLY SAILLISEL, Link up, etc. 116th Bde. attacked in conjunction with 115th Bde. Owing to battle. 10th S.W.B. Left. MESNIL-EN-ARROUAISE in conjunction with 115th Bde. Attack held up East of SAILLY- 2nd R.W.F. right. 17th R.W.F. in support. Attack	EEB
ST. MARTINS WOOD	3rd		Brown withdrew during early morning 115th Bde. knocked SOUTH OF MESNIL-EN-ARROUAISE 17th RWF Right, 10th S.W.B. Left and R.W.F. Support 17th R.W.F. complete position in ST. MARTINS WOOD. 114th Bde. pushed through to advance guard casualties 2 Officers + 30 other ranks.	EEB
do.	4th		17th R.W.F. still in ST. MARTINS WOOD ready to push through to guard through 114th R. Bn. casualties 1 Officer - 6 other ranks.	EEB FM
do.	5th		Remained in same location, relieved by 15th D.L.I. Battn. moved to Brown area between LES BOEUFS + MORVAL Colonel Norman took over command of 2nd R.W.F.	EEB
Bivouac LES BOUEFS	6th		Day spent in cleaning + refitting the Some Battle by the reg'nal Organization of Battn. Works on the morning Div. General visited Battn. + congratulated them Battle Surgs reported	EEB EEB
MORVAL	7th		School hands on the morning boys fired L.Gs. on the range and	EEB SP
do.	8th		afternoon Annual of MGs E.O. Colonel Batty BSO	EEB SR
do.	9th		Lope in range with L.Gs. T.M. demonstration in the afternoon all officers NCOs attended.	EEB

WAR DIARY or INTELLIGENCE SUMMARY

Army Form C. 2118.

Place	Date	Hour	Summary of Events and Information	Remarks and references to Appendices
LECHELLE	10th		Battn. moved up into the neighbourhood of LECHELLE - marched off at 3 p.m.	f.f.f
	11th		Duroon relieved by 17th R.W.F. 115th Bde. relieved by 50th Bde in front line. 17th R.W.F. in centre - relieved by 19th WEST YORKS. Relief completed at 11.50 p.m. C + D Coys in front, B in support, A in Reserve.	f.f.f
	12th		N Zealand Division attacking on left. 'C' Coy S.W.B.'s to capture enemy front line. Attack held up by M.G. fire. Zero attack + 5.25 a.m. 17th R.W.F to push out patrols to ascertain if enemy front line to held or not. No change reported. Casualties 3 O.R.s killed + 15 O.R.s wounded.	f.f.f
	13th	9.50 A.M.	Enemy barrage opened on whole Battn front. Enemy attempted a raid on Right Flank of Right Bgt. + on 2nd R.W.F front. Raid repulsed. Enemy dead seen in our lines. A + B Coys relieved C + B Coys in front line. Casualties 19 O.R.s.	f.f.f
	14th		Day quiet. S.A. brought down on our lines. Casualties 1 officer + 1 O.R.	f.f.f
	15th		Day quiet. Much air activity. Casualties 6 O.R.s (5 gassed)	f.f.f
	16th		Day quiet. Battn. relieved by 13th WELCH - moved out to Bde. in reserve.	f.f.f
			Relief complete at 9.40 p.m.	
Bu Reserve	17th		Day spent in Bde. Reserve. Baths for Battn. B.O. + Coy Commandos reconnoitred positions for Corps Scheme.	f.f.f
	18th		113th + 114th Bdes attacked in conjunction with 5th Divison on the left. 17th Divison on right. Zero at 5.30 a.m. 115th Bde. in Corps Reserve. Battn. moved up to positions at 6.15 a.m. attack succeeded on night but held up on left. Position changed to FARM in the evening.	f.f.f
do.	19th		Day quiet. 115th Bde relieved 114 + 115 Bdes in the line. 17th R.W.F in reserve.	f.f.f
	20th		Battn. relieved by 52nd Bde. of 17th Divison. 17th R.W.F. proceeded to LECHELLE Casualties 1 officer + 6 O.R.s.	f.f.f

WAR DIARY
INTELLIGENCE SUMMARY

Army Form C. 2118.

Place	Date	Hour	Summary of Events and Information	Remarks and references to Appendices
LE TRANSLOY	21st		Batt. marched to billets near LE TRANSLOY. Batt. in huts and under canvas.	
do	22nd		Church parade & reorganisation & cleaning up. Baths allotted to Batt.	
do	23rd		Parades under Coy arrangements including L.G. firing & bayonet fighting. Recreational training in the afternoon.	
do	24th		Parades under Coy arrangements. L.G. training & close order drill. Recreational training in the afternoon.	
do	25th		All Coys on range for musketry. "L.G. practice".	
do	26th		Batt. Batt. carried out a practice in Trench to Trench attack. General recreational training in the afternoon.	
do	27th		All Coys carried out musketry on the range. Recreational training in the afternoon.	
do	28th		Batt. entrained at 1.30 p.m. and arrived at SOREL LE GRANDE at 11.30 pm. Batt. in Huts.	
SOREL-LE-GRANDE	29th		Church parade for the Batt. In readiness to move at an hours notice.	
do	30th		Parades under Coy arrangements including instruction & throwing of German Stick Bombs.	

R.L. Beasley Lt Col
Comdg 17 RWF

WAR DIARY or INTELLIGENCE SUMMARY

Army Form C. 2118.

1/4 W.Y. Vol 35

Place	Date 1918	Hour	Summary of Events and Information	Remarks and references to Appendices
SOREL LE GRANDE	Oct. 1st		Parades under Coy arrangements including L.G. Training & evolution to various Stunts. Station Commanders & Platoon Sgts. attended a Sectional Training Demonstration.	E.E.H.
do.	2nd.		Parades under Coy arrangements. Lewis Gun training & evolution in the afternoon.	E.E.H.
do.	3rd.		Parades under Coy arrangements. Gun training. Batt. in bus area at 7 p.m. Batt. in buses for the night.	E.E.H.
LEMPRIE	4th.		Parades under Coy arrangements. Batt. marched to LEMPRIE arriving at 7 a.m. Batt. marched into the line at BONY and relieved the K.O.Y.L.I. 50th. Division. Relief complete at 9 a.m. Batt. moved into the line at LE CATALET. Dispositions A. B Coys front line C D Coys in support. Relieved the 150th Bde. Relief complete 5 a.m. Casualties 6 OR wounded.	E.E.H. E.E.H.
LE CATALET	5th.		Batt. advanced to a line near AUBENCHEUL AUX BOIS. Casualties 1 Officer wounded 23 OR wounded.	E.E.H.
AUBENCHEUL AUX BOIS	6th.		Batt. in the line. Casualties nil	E.E.H.
do.	7th.		Batt. in the line. Casualties nil	E.E.H.
do.	8th.		Batt. attacked. Zero 1 a.m. Objective BEAUREVOIR LINE and high ground in front of VILLERS OUTREAUX. All objectives taken. About 50 prisoners were taken. Casualties 10 Officers - 120 OR.	E.E.H.
VILLERS OUTREAUX	9th.		Batt. in billets in VILLERS OUTREAUX. Boys carrying out inspection. Casualties nil	E.E.H.
do.	10th.		Batt. marched to billets in CLARY. Complete in billets 7.30 p.m. Casualties nil	E.E.H.
CLARY	11th.		Parades under Coy arrangements. Casualties nil	E.E.H.

Army Form C. 2118.

WAR DIARY
or
INTELLIGENCE SUMMARY.
(Erase heading not required.)

Instructions regarding War Diaries and Intelligence Summaries are contained in F. S. Regs., Part II. and the Staff Manual respectively. Title pages will be prepared in manuscript.

Place	Date	Hour	Summary of Events and Information	Remarks and references to Appendices
CLARY	12th		Battn. marched to billets in TROIS VILLERS. E.O, Adj. and 1 Officer per Coy reconnoitred route to the line. One Officer from H.Qrs. and one per Coy reported to 100th Bde. Hqrs at 6.30 pm.	E.E.H.
TROISVILLERS	13th		Battn. in billets. Took over billets from 2nd R.W.F. casualties 2OR wounded. A.S.B. boys prepared a working party.	E.E.H.
do.	14th		Canadian boy arrangements. A.S.B. boys prepared a working party. Casualties 2OR killed 1OR wounded.	E.E.H.
do.	15th		Canadian boy arrangements. Casualties nil.	E.E.H.
do.	16th		Baths for the Battn. from 01.30 hrs to 15.30 hrs. A.B.+C. Coys provided working parties. Casualties nil.	E.E.H.
do.	17th		Canadian boy arrangements. Casualties nil.	E.E.H.
do.	18th		do. do. do. Working parties provided by A.B+C Coys	E.E.H.
do.	19th		Battn. Battle Surplus Transport + Q.M. Stores personnel paraded for inspection by G.O.C at 3 pm. Casualties nil.	E.E.H.
do.	20th		Battn. marched to position at K.33 central arriving upon the orders of 113th Bde & in reserve. Marched to billets at 5 pm. A.B.+C. Coy complete in billets at 9.40. D Coy left in reserve. Casualties nil.	E.E.H.
do.	21st		E.O. Adj. & 1 Officer per Coy took over from the 13th & 14th R. WELCH in the line. Battn. marched off at 13.00 hrs relief complete at 7.30 pm. Casualties nil.	E.E.H.

WAR DIARY or INTELLIGENCE SUMMARY

Army Form C. 2118.

Place	Date	Hour	Summary of Events and Information	Remarks and references to Appendices
In the line	22nd		Batt. relieved by the 83rd Division. Relief complete at 8pm. Marched back to billets in TROISVILLERS. Complete in billets at 10 pm. Casualties 1 OR killed 3 OR wounded.	E.E.F.
TROISVILLERS	23rd		Batt. moved up in support to 33rd Division at 6 a.m. Batt. following up the 33rd Division. Bivouac for the night near FOREST. Bavillul nil.	E.E.F.
FOREST	24th		Batt. in bivouac near FOREST. The Officers reconnoitred the work. Batt. front. Casualties nil.	E.E.F.
do.	25th		Carriers under boy arrangements. E.O. attended E.O. conference at 12.30 hrs. Casualties nil.	E.E.F.
do.	26th		Batt. relieved the K.R.R. & H.L.I. in the line at ENGLEFONTAINE. Dispositions A & C Coys front line. D. Coy in Support & B Coy in reserve. Relief complete at 8.30 p.m.	E.E.F.
ENGLEFON-TAINE	27th		Enemy put down heavy barrage on our line at 5:30 am under cover of which he attacked. A party of men of the enemy succeeded in getting between our posts but were captured by men of the T.M.B. & 2 S.B. who were sniping at the line. Attack was driven off by all other posts. Casualties 20 OR killed 18 OR wounded & 2 prisoners.	E.E.F.
do.	28th		Quiet day. D. Coy relieved C. Coy in the line. Casualties 1 Officer wounded 2 OR killed 6 OR wounded.	E.E.F.
do.	29th		A, B & D Coys raided the enemy from 0800 hrs to 0900 hrs. Battered from 30 to 40 Germans & killed from 60 to 70 Germans.	E.E.F.

WAR DIARY
or
INTELLIGENCE SUMMARY.
(Erase heading not required.)

Army Form C. 2118.

Place	Date	Hour	Summary of Events and Information	Remarks and references to Appendices
		2p.m.	Battn relieved by 1th R. WELCH FUS from trenches to billets in FOREST. Come pleto in billets 11.30 p.m. 2 Officers wounded. 100R. killed, 670R. wounded, 110R. missing 2 OR NYDN + 20R grased.	4EN. 6EEff. EEf.
FOREST 30R co.	31st		Cards under Bn arrangements. Casualties nil. Cards under Bn arrangements. Casualties nil.	

R.L. Bewley LCol
Commanding 17. R.W.F.
31.10.18

WAR DIARY or INTELLIGENCE SUMMARY

17 RWF Vol 36

Place	Date 1918	Hour	Summary of Events and Information	Remarks and references to Appendices
FOREST	Nov 1st		All officers attended Reconnoitering on wood fighting. Both attacked wood fighting. Reinforcement 3/ORH	
	2nd	9am	B. Reland the 14th Welch in the Englefontaine line. Relief complete at 1830 hrs. Dispositions "B" Coy front line "D" Coy in support "A" & "C" Coys in Echelon nr ENGLEFONTAINE. Casualties 1 off. wounded.	
ENGLEFONTAINE	3rd		Quiet day. Casualties nil.	
	4th		Battalion attacked at 6.15am in conjunction with 2nd R.W.F. & 10th R.W.F. Objective a position E of FOREST DE MORMAL. All objectives gained. Casualties 1 Offr killed, 3 Officers wounded, 3 O.R. killed, 41 O.R. wounded. The 113th Brigade moved through us at 0800 hrs. Battalion occupied the old front line for the night.	
	5th		Batt in ENGLEFONTAINE. Under an hours notice to move. Casualties nil. Reinforcements 116 O.R. + 2 Officers	
	6th		Batt. received orders to proceed to western edge of FOREST DE MORMAL & Battalion proceeded to BIRLEMONT for dinner. Casualties 1 Officer wounded.	
MOLHAIN STATION	7th		11:30am Bn bivouacked to billets at MOLHAIN STATION.	
	8th		At 7.30 am Bn marched to the village POT DE VIN & awaited orders to bring Bn to the ready. Bn was ordered to be at Maubeuge to attack on the enemy if the Bn was reported to be thoroughly held by the enemy. At 11am the Bn was reported to return to billets at MOLHAIN STATION	35 p

WAR DIARY
or
INTELLIGENCE SUMMARY

Army Form C. 2118.

Place	Date 1918	Hour	Summary of Events and Information	Remarks and references to Appendices
AULNOYE STATION	Nov 9th	10 am	Bn remained in billets at AULNOYE STATION.	
		9am to 12 noon	Bn did a practice route march. 2pm to 4pm recreational training.	
			25610 Cpl G.R. Roberts awarded Bar to Military Medal and 26162 Pte H. Jones " " Military Medal for bravery in the field.	
		11th	At 11 am report of heavy gun-fire was heard & bugles in the village sounded the "cease fire" from that time rung north would no sound was heard. Moral Bn. prisoners were carried out during the remainder of the day. The Bn was staffed as follows:—	
			Commanding Battalion C.O. Lt Col R.R. Bewsher D.S.O. 2nd in C°	
			Major T. Preston M.C. Adjutant Capt A.N. Knoll	
			2nd Lt N. Dixon 2 Intelligence Officer 2 Lt E.J. Floyd	
			Q.M. 2nd Lieut T.J. Jones M.C. Transport Officer Lt R.J. Jones	
			C. "A" Coy Capt R.T. Jones 3 "C" Coy Capt D. Thurston	
			2/Lt E.H. Archer 2 "B" Coy Capt G.A. Shingleton	
			2/Lt Bates under CoL arrangements including class were held	
			x R.C. Cinema. 2pm to 4pm recreational training	
	12th			
	13th		Battalion drill by the C.O. 2pm to 4pm recreational training	

WAR DIARY
or
INTELLIGENCE SUMMARY.
(Erase heading not required.)

Army Form C. 2118.

Place	Date 1918	Hour	Summary of Events and Information	Remarks and references to Appendices
AUNO/E STATION	Nov 14th		9am to 12noon Brigade route march. 2pm 4pm Recreational training	
	15th	10am to 12noon Inspection of Coys by Commanding Officer. 2pm to 4pm Recreational Training.		
	16th		Capt R.D. Shenah & Lt N.D. Baslar & Lt. Bishop awarded Military Cross for services in the field. 25781 Sgt O. Lucas M.M. awarded D.C.M. for services in the field. Church service held throughout the day. No Parades.	
	17th		The following honours & awards for bravery in the field. 39 C.M.R. 13th & 14th M.M. 264438 Pte L.H. Bentz. Military Medal. 25898 L/Cpl W. Davis 42846 Pte J.R. Taylor. 26180 Pte T. Rowlands 31109 Cpl R. Thomas 59747 Sgt G.F. Colbas 26396 Sgt S. Capp & Coy arrangements. Parades under Coy arrangements. 2pm 6.4pm	
	18th		9am to 12noon Parades under Coy arrangement. 2pm 4pm recreational training Brigade route march.	
	19th		9.30am to 12.30pm Kingscourt. 16 OR Parades under Coy arrangement including Box Order Drill. Training 2pm 4pm inspecting transport. 54457 Cpl A. Linton awarded M. Medal for services in the field. England ton to march.	
	20th		9am to 12noon Parades under Coy arrangements. R.G. training 2pm to 4pm inspection of transport. 2pm 4pm Recreational training	

WAR DIARY or INTELLIGENCE SUMMARY.

Army Form C. 2118.

(Erase heading not required.)

Place	Date 1918	Hour	Summary of Events and Information	Remarks and references to Appendices
AMIENS STATION	22nd	9am to 12 noon	Close order drill & L.G. training under Coy arrangements.	
		2pm to 4pm	Recreational training.	
	23rd		Bns allotted to B. Brigade's Holiday. W. 10am. Bn attended Medal Ribbon Presentation by Major General T. Cabell. 2pm to 4pm recreational training.	
	24th	9.30am	Of & A Mixed inspecting Military Medal on bravery in the field. Church Parade held throughout the day. Bns allotted to B. for 2pm to 4pm	
	25th	0830-1100 hrs	recreational training	
		9am to 12 noon	Bn to Coy arrangements	for 1 to 4pm
	26th	9.30am to 12 noon	Brigade route march 2pm to 4pm recreational training	
			Compliment to 1 Officer	
	27th		Supernumerary under Coy arrangements to attend under Coy L.G. training. Conference to Jaro 250K.	
		2pm to 4pm	recreational training	
	28th	9am to 12 noon	Bn parade under Coy arrangements vehicle	
			Close order drill & L.G. training	Major & Capt Bisgood, Coy Gunty Lt.
			field regmts not O.R. WS 2nd Lt. 13rd 2nd Lt. R.E. Ross	
	29th	9am to 12 noon	Bn parade under Coy arrangements for 2pm to 4pm recreational training	
	30th	9am to 12 noon	Bn at disposal of Coy Commander 2pm to 4pm recreational training	

P. Welton Major
Commanding 1/4 Bn

Army Form C. 2118.

17 RWF
Vol 37

WAR DIARY
INTELLIGENCE SUMMARY.
(Erase heading not required.)

Instructions regarding War Diaries and Intelligence Summaries are contained in F. S. Regs., Part II. and the Staff Manual respectively. Title pages will be prepared in manuscript.

Place	Date	Hour	Summary of Events and Information	Remarks and references to Appendices
AULNOYE STATION	DEC 1918 1st		Church Parades held throughout the day.	No
	2nd	9am to 12 noon	Parades under company arrangements. 2pm 6.4pm recreational training.	No
	3rd		His Majesty the King passed through AULNOYE at 11am. The Battalion formed up on the Estain, side of the PETIT MAUBEUGE road. 2pm to 4pm recreational training.	No
	4th		25346 Pte E.D. Hughes awarded the Military Medal for bravery in the field. 9am to 12noon Parades under Coy arrangements. 2pm to 4.30pm recreational training.	No
	5th	9.30am to 12.30pm	Brigade route march. 2pm to 4.30pm recreational training.	No
	6th	9am to 12noon	Parades under Coy arrangements. 2pm to 4.30pm recreational training.	No
			2 officers joined the battalion as reinforcements.	
	7th	9am to 12noon	Parades under Coy arrangements. During the morning the Acting Brigadier Commanding inspected all billets. 2pm to 4.4pm recreational training. 8 O.R's joined the battalion as reinforcements.	No 36P to 4 sheets
	8th		Baths allotted to battalion throughout the day. Moral Church service held. Parades under Coy arrangements. 2pm to 4pm	No
	9th	9am to 12 noon	recreational training	

WAR DIARY
INTELLIGENCE SUMMARY
(Erase heading not required.)

Army Form C. 2118.

Place	Date	Hour	Summary of Events and Information	Remarks and references to Appendices
AULNOYE STATION	1918 Jan 10th	9am to 12.30pm	Battalion route march. 2pm to 4pm recreational training.	
"	11th		During the morning Coys were inspected by the Brigadier General as follows: A Coy marching order. B Coy Kit & Billet Inspection in billets. C Coy Turnout, wearing of greatcoats, Rifle, Belt & Bayonet. D Coy & Platoon Drill. 2pm to 4pm recreational training	
"	12th		The following decorations awarded for services in the field. Lieut Col R.P. Beasley D.S.O. 2nd Bar to D.S.O. Capt E.A. Livingston Military Cross Capt D.J. Giles " " 93067 Sjt J.N. Burns Distinguished Conduct Medal 54621 L.Cpl J.P. Jones " " 9am to 12 noon Parades under Coy arrangements. 2pm to 4pm recreational training.	
"	13th	9am to 12.30pm	Battalion route march. 2pm to 4pm recreational training.	
"	14th	9am to 12 noon	Parades under Coy arrangements. 2pm to 4pm recreational training by Coys throughout the day.	
"	15th		Church service field throughout the day.	
"	16th	9am to 12 noon	Parades under Coy arrangements including musketry 2pm to 4pm recreational training. 17 O.R's joined the Battalion as reinforcements	

WAR DIARY / INTELLIGENCE SUMMARY

Army Form C. 2118.

Place	Date	Hour	Summary of Events and Information	Remarks and references to Appendices
AULNOYE STATION	DEC 1918 17th	9am to 12.30pm	Parade under Coy arrangements including musketry. 2pm to 4pm recreational training.	
"	18th	9am to 12.30pm	Parade under Coy arrangements including musketry. 2pm to 4pm recreational training. 26 OR's joined the Battalion as reinforcements.	
"	19th	9am to 12.30pm	Parade under Coy arrangements. 2pm to 4pm recreational training.	
"	20th	9am to 12.30pm	Brigade route march. 2pm to 4pm recreational training.	
"	21st		Battn allotted to the battalion during the day. The G.O.C. inspected transport on the lines at 10.45 hours. 2/Lt. L. Col. J. Kenhe and 56915 Pte G.J. Bass awarded Divisional Certificates for Gallantry. Massed Bands & Drums of 115th Infantry Brigade played Retreat in open opposite Aubrage Hotel at 16.00 hrs.	
"	22nd		Church services. Later throughout the day.	
"	23rd	9am to 12.30pm	Brigade route march. 2pm to 4pm recreational training.	
"	24th		Battalion ao Coy arrangements 6 OR's joined the Battalion as reinforcements.	
"	25th		Church services. All through the day. Xmas Dinner served at 1pm. Sergts. & Drs. Orchestra was in attendance.	

Army Form C. 2118.

WAR DIARY
of
INTELLIGENCE SUMMARY.
(Erase heading not required.)

Instructions regarding War Diaries and Intelligence Summaries are contained in F. S. Regs., Part II. and the Staff Manual respectively. Title pages will be prepared in manuscript.

Place	Date 1918	Hour	Summary of Events and Information	Remarks and references to Appendices
AULNOYE STATION	Dec 26th	9am to 12.30pm	Coy's at disposal of Coy Commanders. Battalion fell into Brigade cross country competition/also Cup final. 2.30 to 4pm recreational.	
"	27th	9am to 12.30pm	Brigade route march. 2pm to 4pm recreational. Training.	
"	28th	9am to 12.30pm	Coy's at disposal of O.C. Coy's. 2pm to 4pm recreational training.	
ENGEFONTAINE	29th		Battalion marched to Engefontaine & billeted.	
INCHY	30th		At 9am battalion proceeded to Inchy & billeted there for the night.	
	31st		The battalion entrained at 7.30am and proceeded to camp near Blangy Tronville.	

E. A. Skington Capt.
Commanding 14th P.W.Vo.

HQrs 115 Inf Bde

17th BATTALION
No. 7228
Date 2.3.19
Royal Welsh Fusiliers

Herewith War Diary of this
Unit for the month of Feb. 1919.

S.T. Phillips Lieut
for O.C. 17 R.W.F.

WAR DIARY
INTELLIGENCE SUMMARY.
(Erase heading not required.)

Army Form C. 2118.

17 RWF

Place	Date	Hour	Summary of Events and Information	Remarks and references to Appendices
BLANGY TRONVILLE	1919 JAN 1st		Companies on fatigue all day in the camp	No
	2nd	9am to 10.15am	Ceremonial drill under Coy arrangements	No
		10.15am to 12.30pm	Coys employed in brushing parade ground. Banking up huts	
	3rd		Battalion on work of camp	No
	4th	9am to 10am	Close order drill under Coy arrangements	No
		10am to 12.30pm	Banking up huts & laying French boards	
	5th	9am to 12.30pm	Parades under Coy arrangements	No
	to		and reconstruction of camp	
		2pm to 6pm	Recreational training	No
	30th		Honours for service in the field. The New Years Honours Gazette	
			Captn R.F. Hearly Military Cross	
			241692 Lt Beck J.E. Distinguished Conduct Medal	
			25123 C.Q.M.S. Atkinson E. Meritorious Service Medal	
			203PO C.Q.M.S. Owen T.W.	
			Captn A/Col Lewis — Mentioned in Dispatches	
		26109 A/Col Jones R.J. — Mentioned in Dispatches	

R.L. Beasley Lt Col
Commanding 17th RWF

WAR DIARY
INTELLIGENCE SUMMARY

Army Form C. 2118.

17 RW F 5 I
98l 39
88G
2 sheets

Place	Date	Hour	Summary of Events and Information	Remarks and references to Appendices
BLANGY TRONVILLE	1919 JAN 10th		The King's Colour was presented to the battalion by the G.O.C. Div (Major General T.A. Cubitt). On arrival in the camp after being played round the camp before being placed in the Officers Mess.	No
"	FEB 1st	9am to 12.30pm	Parades were ordinary arrangements and work on camp improvements. Educational classes held during the morning. 2pm to 5pm recreational training.	No
"	6th		H.R.H. the Prince of Wales paid the Battalion an informal visit & inspected the camp during the morning.	No
"	7th 8th	9am to 12.30pm	Parades were Company arrangements & camp improvements. Educational classes held during the morning. 2pm to 5pm recreational training.	No
"	9th 13th		The Battalion marched to QUERRIEU to view the shield Presented to H.R.H. the Prince of Wales.	No
"	14th		Parades were Company arrangements & work on camp improvements during the morning.	No
"	15th 25th	2pm to 4pm	Every Royal Classes held during the morning. Recreational training.	No

R.L. Beasley
Commanding 17th R.W. Surrey

To O in C
 / 115 Inf Bde

Herewith Original Copy of War
Diary of this Unit for the
month of March 1919.
Please acknowledge receipt.

E. Morgan Lieut
for O/C R.W.F

Army Form C. 2118.

WAR DIARY
or
INTELLIGENCE SUMMARY.
(Erase heading not required.)

Instructions regarding War Diaries and Intelligence Summaries are contained in F. S. Regs., Part II. and the Staff Manual respectively. Title pages will be prepared in manuscript.

Place	Date 1919	Hour	Summary of Events and Information	Remarks and references to Appendices
BLANGY TRONVILLE	March 1	9 am to 12.30 pm 2 pm to 5 pm	Men worked on Camp improvements Recreational training the day Church service held throughout the day	A.J. A.J.
	2nd			
	3rd	9 am to 11.15 am 11.15 to 12.15 pm 2 pm to 4 pm	Parades under Coy arrangements Educational class Recreational training Battn allotted to the Battalion	A.J.
	4th	6 pm		A.J.
	5th			
	6th			
	7/10	9 am to 12.30 pm 2.6 pm to 4 pm	Parades under Coy arrangements Recreational training	A.J.
	11th			
			Church services held throughout the day	A.J.
	15			
	16th		Parades under Coy arrangements 9 am to 12.30 pm 2 pm to 4 pm. Recreational training	A.J.
	17th			
	21st		The battalion moved from present location to huts allotted them in the 2nd R.N.F Camp	A.J.
	22nd			
			Church services held throughout the day	A.J.
	23rd			
	24/27	9 am to 12.30 pm 2 pm to 4 pm	Men worked on Coy camp improvements	A.J.
	28/29		" " Recreational training	A.J.

WAR DIARY
or
INTELLIGENCE SUMMARY.
(Erase heading not required.)

Army Form C. 2118.

Place	Date	Hour	Summary of Events and Information	Remarks and references to Appendices
BLANGY TRONVILLE	1919 MARCH 28th		235340 Pte Hobson G awarded Medaille Militaire 3rd Class for services in the field.	
	29th	9am to 12.30pm	Men worked on camp improvements	
		9am to 12.30pm 2pm to 5pm	Men worked on camp improvements	
	30th		Church services held throughout the day.	
	3rd	9am to 12.30pm 2pm to 5pm	Men worked on camp improvements & Recreational training.	

E.O. Shingleton Captain
Commanding 19th R.D.

WAR DIARY
or
INTELLIGENCE SUMMARY.

Army Form C. 2118.

17 R.W.F.
Vol 4

Place	Date 1919	Hour	Summary of Events and Information	Remarks and references to Appendices
Blangy Tronville	April 1st		Baths at GLISY from 13.00 to 15.00 hrs. Educational class 1 hr.	
	16 2nd		Bn. wood carrying for camp. Educational class 1 hr	
	4"		Church services throughout the day.	
	5"		Route March to VILLERS BRETONNEUX. Dress - Drill Order. 2 off. 1 O.R. for Disposal.	
	6"			
	7"		Bn. carrying wood for camp. Educational class 1 hour	
	10"			
	11"		Church services throughout the day.	
	12"		Route March. Dress: Drill Order. 1 off. 2 O.R. for Disposal.	
	13"			
	14"		Bn. carrying wood. Educational class 1 hr. Lt. Col. R.J. Beazley proceeded to command 50 Labour Group. Boulogne.	
	15"			
	16"		Bn. on Wood Fatigue. Educational class 1 hr.	
	17"		Good Friday. Church service throughout the day.	

Army Form C. 2118.

WAR DIARY
or
INTELLIGENCE SUMMARY.
(Erase heading not required.)

Instructions regarding War Diaries and Intelligence Summaries are contained in F. S. Regs, Part II. and the Staff Manual respectively. Title pages will be prepared in manuscript.

Place	Date	Hour	Summary of Events and Information	Remarks and references to Appendices
BLANGY TRONVILLE	18th		Bn on wood carrying. Educational class 1 hr.	(B)
	19th		Church Services throughout the day	(NC)
	20th to 25th		Bn on wood Fatigue. Educational classes 1 hr. each day. Maj. J.A. Wilson M.C. assumed command of Bn. from 113th Bde. Capt EP Ewing a/a M.C. to be P.O.W. (23.4.19.)	(B)
	26th		Church Services throughout the day.	
	28th to 30th		Bn on wood Fatigue. Maj. J.A. Wilson M.C. to France.	(B)

N.T. Heneage Lieut
for O.C. 17 Bn. Royal Welsh Fus

www.ingramcontent.com/pod-product-compliance
Lightning Source LLC
Chambersburg PA
CBHW080915230426
43667CB00015B/2685